T0380791

THE
SECOND COMING
OF THE
MESSIAH

Will Not Be in Your Generation!
But Who's? A Journal for Followers of Jesus

REVEREND TONDALA L. HAYWARD

WESTBOW
PRESS®
A DIVISION OF THOMAS NELSON
& ZONDERVAN

WestBow Press books may be ordered through booksellers or by contacting:

WestBow Press
A Division of Thomas Nelson & Zondervan
1663 Liberty Drive
Bloomington, IN 47403
www.westbowpress.com
844-714-3454

Common English Bible (CEB)
Copyright © 2011 by Common English Bible

ISBN: 979-8-3850-2723-1 (sc)
ISBN: 979-8-3850-2724-8 (e)

Library of Congress Control Number: 2024911805

Print information available on the last page.

WestBow Press rev. date: 06/18/2024

CONTENTS

CONTENTS

INTRODUCTION

When God calls you to do something, sometimes you ask yourself, *Why me?* I've asked myself that question over and over and over and over. Probably a couple of hundred times or more. However, I keep getting the same answer from God: *Why not you? It's your heart.* After many reflections, I learned God can use anybody to do God's will if you have a heart after God and not humanity. In other words, we need to do the will of the Creator and not the created. It sounds simple, right? Well, simple can be complex at times. Let's take a gander at the story of Noah in Genesis.

In Genesis 6, Noah experienced the complexity in doing the will of God, when God became displeased with humanity. I'm sure people teased Noah while he built the ark because of its dimensions. They couldn't imagine the earth would get enough floodwaters to float the ark. We didn't get details on the reactions of the people, while Noah was constructing the ark. Together, we can imagine that it wasn't a yacht. I'm imagining a cruise ship with AD as its title (*Anno Domini*—in the year of the Lord). However, there weren't amenities, which means no running water, buffets, 24-hour room service, luxurious rooms, and entertainment. Instead, the view was a flood with all its ramifications. There wasn't an ocean view.

If the ark was being built in society today, people would come from miles around to observe its construction. They would ask questions and take pictures to put on social media. Therefore, I think it's safe to say Noah had a crowd of observers, who may have told others to "come and see what Noah is building!" Do you think he told his observers God told him to build it? Did Noah mention to anyone that there was going to be a flood? If he did, they may have thought he was mentally ill. I'm sure he told his family since they boarded the ark. Who do you think helped Noah gather pairs of animals? More importantly, who helped him build the ark? You see, the Bible isn't always detail inclusive. Sometimes, we must read between the lines to get a full interpretation of Scripture. Do you think his family assisted in the construction? God hasn't said anything to me about the construction of the ark. I'm just pondering. But this is what I do know: GOD WAS WITH NOAH!

Noah was in his right mind when he built the ark. After all, God said he was righteous. This is what God told Noah, when he received his assignment: "I am now bringing the floodwaters over the earth to destroy everything under the sky that breathes. Everything on earth is about to take its7 last breath. But I will set up my covenant with you. You will go into the ark together with your sons, your wife, and your sons' wives. From all living things—from all creatures—you are to bring a pair, male and female, into the ark with you to keep them alive" (Genesis 6:17-19).

Thus, we may never know the whole truth regarding all of the correspondences between Noah, God, and Noah's relatives; however, we do believe God told Noah to build an enormous ark. In Genesis 6:13-16 God said to Noah, "The end has come for all creatures, since they have filled the earth with violence. I am now about to destroy them along with the earth, so make a wooden ark. Make the ark with nesting places and cover it inside and out with tar. This is how you should make it: four hundred fifty feet long, seventy-five feet wide, and forty-five feet high. Make a roof for the ark and complete it one foot from the top. Put a door in its side. In the hold below, make the second and third decks."

It probably took years for Noah to build the ark. The Bible doesn't give the timeframe, which is understandable because the Bible can't contain every story and relate every detail to us. If it did, we couldn't carry it around because of its weight. However, we do know Noah was 600 years old when the floodwaters came. God allowed it to rain 40 days and 40 nights. People may have trekked to the ark to be saved, but Noah did everything as our Lord asked. Of what we know, his family were the only humans allowed on the ark. They may have gone below deck so that they couldn't hear the wailing and feel less of their emotions from the destruction. Noah's faithfulness to God made him and his family worthy of being saved.

After many reflections of how God uses ordinary people to complete tasks that gives glory to God, I realized I am worthy of being used by God in extraordinary ways. God used Noah to build an ark when humanity decided to use their freewill to obey Satan and not their Creator-God. From Noah's experience, we learned God won't destroy creation by water again. Therefore, when we see a rainbow in the heavenly skies, it reassures us of God's promise.

Again, I imagine people flocked to Noah's Ark apologizing for their disobedience. They wanted to be saved. However, it wasn't up to Noah to make that decision. It was the decision of our

Creator as to whether who would be saved when the land became a sea of water. Some people believe God's reaction to humanity's disobedience was cruel. But the reality is many of us believe consequences are warranted. Thus, how long should God offer us the free gift of grace? Write your reflection on the line.

_____

God doesn't put a time limit on grace; however, we shouldn't take advantage of it.

The Truth is: God has plans for us that are different from what we can envision. Have you been seeking God's plans for your life?

_____

I've sought God for my future. It's more than I can encompass with my human cognitive abilities. God is going to enlarge my territory. I never thought praying the prayer of Jabez would lead me to preaching and teaching a multitude. I didn't graduate with honors, nor do I know the Bible from cover to cover. Plus, I'm an introvert. I thrive in an introvert world: solitude, discerning, praying, planning, talking to myself and listening to God. I say that I'm a learned extrovert. I learned some extrovert characteristics to develop my personality. But first, I had to learn more about my introvert character to intertwine it with the life of an extrovert. Now, I'm an ambivert, which is someone whose overall personality is between introversion and extraversion. I love solitude, and I love being a social butterfly. Thus, I've found my happy medium.

Are you an introvert, ambivert, or extrovert? _____

How do you know? _____

THE PRAYER OF JABEZ

When you pray the Prayer of Jabez, you will need to be ready for transformation. Do you know the Prayer of Jabez? If not, I'll tell you about it. If you do, you're getting a refresher. Here's the scripture in 1 Chronicles 4:

Jabez was more honored than his brothers. His mother had named him Jabez, saying, "I bore him in pain." Jabez called on Israel's God: "If only you would greatly bless me and increase my territory. May your power go with me to keep me from trouble, so as not to cause me pain." And God granted his request.

There's a little book at our favorite bookstore, Amazon, called *The Prayer of Jabez* by Bruce Wilkerson. I received mine in 2014, when I graduated from Memphis Theological Seminary in Tennessee. The principal at Lowrance Elementary School gave it to me as a gift. Yes, I'm a licensed elementary teacher. I taught school while attending seminary, married and with children. WHEW! I SURVIVED!!

When I opened the book, I found these handwritten words on the back of the front cover….

> *Tondala,*
>
> *"I pray that points a clear picture of His perfect will for your life through reading this book. Open your heart, mind, and spirit to what He's saying. I'm convinced that He is going to absolutely blow your mind."*
>
> *Sincerely,*
> *Kevin Bates*
> *4/30/14*

I thought, *What a gift!* I felt the personal touch from his gift because he addressed me as Tondala not Ms. Hayward. In a school environment, we usually address each other by our last name to teach the students to do the same. I've been praying this prayer, and God has blessed me indeed. I really don't expect God's blessings to stop now! In fact, I'm anticipating more will come. Thank you, Mr. Bates, for this little reminder of how God wants us to be prosperous.

Let's talk about Jabez:

In Chronicles, the chronicler stopped telling us about the generations of Judah to tell us about Jabez, who was an honorable person with an unsentimental name. Imagine being called Jabez and when people see you, they say, "Here comes pain walking down the road." Your friends would blame all their mistakes and burdens on you because you're the "Here Comes the Trouble" person. Name origins in ancient days were meaningful. I have a unique name. How many people do you know with the name Tondala? Also, how many people do you know name

Chimika? I believe my mom, Barbara Ann, and her stepsister, Faye, get an A+ for accomplishing their task of naming their children with unique first names. I don't know the meaning of our names. But Jabez name means pain; however, he overcame the upset of his painstaking name through prayer. God blessed him abundantly. Bruce Wilkinson writes, "Jabez was blessed simply because he refused to let any obstacle, person, or opinion loom larger than God's nature. And God's nature is to bless" (p. 29).

I would like to ask you to read the Scripture and pray the "Prayer of Jabez" You can add words to this prayer to make it more personal.

Are you going to do it? If yes, when? _____

If no, why not? _____

Also, buy the book so that you'll gain a deeper understanding of "The Prayer of Jabez."

SAYING YES TO GOD DOESN'T MEAN YOU'RE A GENIUS

As you pray the Prayer of Jabez God will reveal God's plans for your life. The next statement I'm going to say is crucial.

> *You don't have to know everything to say yes to God-when God calls you to be the hands and feet of Jesus. Because God will equip you with a backpack of tools and resources for the journey. And each time you need help, God will tell you to scour through your backpack of gifts, talents, skills, and graces to pull out what you need. Sometimes, you may need to call a follower of Jesus to help you stay on your journey. However, calling for help, means you're ready to be vulnerable.*

Are you ready to share your struggles with others?

_____

Well, I will share my struggles with you...

As a person called to preach, teach, and use my prophetic voice, I realized knowing the Bible from the front to the back wasn't a pre- or post- requirement. Therefore, since I didn't know the Bible from cover to cover, I questioned my call. Many times, I asked myself, *How could I minister or even pastor people who are older than me?* I felt they have been reading the Bible longer than I have. But the Spirit of God awakened me and helped me to realize age isn't nothing but a number when it backs up to faith.

God wants us to come humbly with childlike faith. The Gospels tell us Jesus rebuked the Apostles when parents brought their children to him so that he could lay hands on them and pray for them. He told them, "Allow the children to come to me …. Don't forbid them because the kingdom of heaven belongs to people like these children." Then he blessed the children and went away from there (Matthew 19:14-15). What did we learn from Jesus's demand of the children coming to see him, in an era where children were expected to sit down, be at their parents' beck and call, and be as quiet as mice? After much reflection, we should learn that we need to have childlike faith. We need to come humble and vulnerable to Jesus so that we can surrender to our Lord and Master.

Sometimes surrendering to the will of God is a daunting task. Why? It gets us out of our comfort zone. At times, it requires us to embrace new concepts and venture on unexpected journeys. But running away from the will of God only works for a little while. It isn't everlasting! Either we'll submit to the Lord's authority in the earthly kingdom or in the heavenly kingdom.

Romans 14:8-12 reminds us, *"If we live, we live for the Lord, and if we die, we die for the Lord. Therefore, whether we live or die, we belong to God. This is why Christ died and lived: so that he might be Lord of both the dead and the living. But why do you judge your brother or sister? Or why do you look down on your brother or sister? We all will stand in front of the judgment seat of God. Because it is written…*

'As I live, says the Lord, every knee will bow to me, and every tongue will give praise to God. So then, each of us will give an account of ourselves to God.'"

I assume we want to submit to God on earth to ensure we have lived a righteous life on earth in order to dwell in heaven. Either way, we will submit. If you don't believe it, then you must've forgotten about Jonah. If you haven't heard this biblical story or need me to refresh your memory, please keep reading or listening to hear more about Jonah.

A SUMMARY OF JONAH NEGLECTING TO DO GOD'S WILL

Jonah didn't want to go to Nineveh to deliver a message from the Lord about their sinful nature. Instead, he ran and got on a ship to Tarshish, which was located on a port in Joppa. To help bring Jonah to his senses, the Lord sent a mighty storm while he was on the ship. The treacherous storm made the captain and his sailors pray to their gods so that the mighty winds wouldn't destroy the ship. Jonah was sleeping downstairs, which is something we usually do when we run from God. We try to sleep our troubles away. Did this sound familiar? Are you like me in trying to sleep your troubles away?

I don't know about you, but I try to sleep or become a busy bee at doing other discipleship tasks instead of what God wants me to do at that particular time. For instance, I begin to plan ministry tasks to do at church or for the community. We're supposed to be the hands and feet of Christ, RIGHT? I may read an inspirational book or the Bible because knowledge is power, RIGHT? Unfortunately, it's not the power journey I should be embarking upon at that moment. At times I've called the sick and shut-ins and checked in with those whom I'm counseling. After all, showing love to my neighbors by loving your neighbor as yourself is one of the greatest commandments, RIGHT?

But I believe that I was substituting one task for another and another. Also, my DIY projects or gardening became a priority. I would plan to work on the will of God after I finished my assumed important tasks, but I would be pooped. Hesitation leads Procrastination, which doesn't lead us to a Destination.

God told me "Procrastination is UnGodliness."

Wow, oh my! Did we believe getting engage in presumably essential tasks make any sense? I'm telling you from experience: NO!! Running from God never works! God is omniscient—all knowing— and omnipresent—present everywhere at the same time. Therefore, we can't play hide and seek with God because God knows what we're thinking and our whereabouts. If you don't believe me, let's finish summarizing Jonah.

As the winds became more treacherous, when Jonah was on the ship, the captain woke Jonah up so that he could pray to God. Eventually the sailors decided to cast lots to reveal who brought this danger upon them. Jonah 1:8-12 tells us the lot fell on Jonah. They asked Jonah, "What do you do and where are you from? What's your country and of what people are you?" He said to them, "I'm a Hebrew. I worship the Lord, the God of heaven—who made the sea and the dry land." Then the men were terrified and said to him, "What have you done?" The men knew that Jonah was fleeing from the Lord because he had told them. They said to him, "What will we do about you so that the sea will become calm around us?" The sea was continuing to rage. He said to them, "Pick me up and hurl me into the sea! Then the sea will become calm around you. I know it's my fault that this great storm has come upon you" CEB).

Of course, the men refused to hurl Jonah over the side of the boat. Thus, after the continuous raging of the storms, they prayed and asked God to forgive them of their actions. The trained sailors had no other choice but to toss Jonah overboard. When Jonah's body touched the raging sea, the storm stopped.

But the sea didn't swallow Jonah. **HE SURVIVED!** How did he survive treacherous waters that were meant to rock some sense into him?

God provided a whale to swallow him up. He stayed in the belly of the whale for three days and three nights praying to God. These are the words of Jonah to God:

> I called out to the Lord in my distress, and he answered me.
>   From the belly of the underworld, I cried out for help;
>   you have heard my voice.
> You had cast me into the depths in the heart of the seas,
>   and the flood surrounds me.
>   All your strong waves and rushing water passed over me.
> So, I said, 'I have been driven away from your sight.
>   Will I ever again look on your holy temple?
> Waters have grasped me to the point of death;
>   the deep surrounds me.
> Seaweed is wrapped around my head
>
>   at the base of the undersea mountains.
> I have sunk down to the underworld;
>   its bars held me with no end in sight.
>   But you brought me out of the pit.'

When my endurance was weakening,
* I remembered the Lord,*
and my prayer came to you,
* to your holy temple.*
Those deceived by worthless things lose their chance for mercy.
But me, I will offer a sacrifice to you with a voice of thanks.
* That which I have promised, I will pay.*
* Deliverance belongs to the Lord!*
Then the Lord spoke to the fish, and it vomited Jonah onto the dry land
(Jonah 2:1-10).

Jonah prayed in the belly of the whale. God heard his prayers! This is one of many examples of how God hears our prayers even when we are in the depths of the sea. After Jonah's whale of an experience, he submitted to the will of God by going to Ninevah to deliver the message from God. Like Jonah, I learned the hard way that you can't sprint or long-distance run from God. I guess this is why I spend my time in the wee hours of the morning writing this book. The Spirit of my Lord wakes me and whispers, *The book*. Thus, I can't sleep because of the tasks God wants me to complete keep rambling in my mind. I've learned that when I submit to the authority of God, those sleepless mornings become joyful new every day mornings. As I write, my faith in myself and God increases. The Holy Spirit is guiding me to put God's words on paper for the children of God. My faith increases with each thought, word, sentence, and paragraph. I'm becoming complete. Therefore, I truly understand Lamentations 3:22-23, which says, "Certainly the faithful love of the Lord hasn't ended; certainly, God's compassion isn't through! They are renewed every morning. Great is your faithfulness."

"Great is Thy Faithfulness" by Thomas O. Chisholm is one of my favorite hymns. I'm an ole school and contemporary music Christian gal. I love hymns and modern music. Contemporary Christian music has a nice beat, and I love connecting the words to real time. The hymns remind me of my foundation. When I hear and sing hymns, I reminiscence on the past. I visualize myself as the little girl who rocked from side to side while the adults sang. When I learned the lyrics, I joined them. I would say, I want the music to move me like it moved my Aunt Ollie, Uncle Bill, the pastor, and others. At that young age, I didn't realize the movement was the Holy Spirit moving inside of them, which made tears flow, hands clap and raise, and bodies lift with praise hands raised to our Heavenly Father. I knew they felt something different in which I began to eventually seek as I became older. Little did I know the Holy Spirit was already living inside of me. I just needed to release the third person of the Trinity. I needed to not be afraid of others thinking I'm too holy. Most importantly, I needed to learn the Holy Spirit empowers, equips, and guides me to righteous living.

Over the years, I've learned to appreciate and give thanks to all the Holy Spirit has to offer. I also thank you, God, for your unconditional love and compassion that you always show me despite my actions. I thank you for the grace you always render to me even though I don't deserve it. I thank you for your mercy because you don't give me what I am due instead you give me the greatest gift of all: charity, which is the highest form of LOVE!

My Brothers and Sisters in Christ, what God does for me, God will do the same thing for you. Therefore, accept the love, compassion, grace, and mercy that God offers to you that are new every morning. *Great is Thy Faithfulness.*

CHAPTER ONE

THE PROPHETIC CALL

Sometimes prophets have a difficult time accepting their call from God to deliver messages to people. I am one of them! As you can see, I RAN! My plight reminds me of Jonah and Moses. I didn't get swallowed up in a whale, but I've had stormy nights in which I couldn't sleep. Sometimes, I'll wake to the sound of God calling my name, a dream, or the dreaded middle of the night trip to the bathroom, which left me awake tossing, turning, and thinking about the will of God for my life. Why was I troubled? FEAR!

I felt like Moses. Who would believe me? He didn't have enough self-worth. Moses thought he didn't have the cognitive abilities needed to lead God's people. That was my main issue. I felt I wasn't ready to do God's work, especially in prophetic ministry. I had no problem with helping others. But I guess I didn't realize helping others by delivering messages from God is the purpose and mission of prophets.

I told you about Jonah on the run and his whale of an experience. Now let me tell you about Moses. God wanted to send Moses to Egypt to rescue the Israelites from captivity. Their conversation went like this:

> But Moses said to God, "Who am I to go to Pharaoh and to bring the Israelites out of Egypt?" God said, "I'll be with you. And this will show you that I'm the one who sent you. After you bring the people out of Egypt, you will come back here and worship God on this mountain. But Moses said to God, "If I now come to the Israelites and say to them, 'The God of your ancestors has sent me to you,' they are going to ask

me, 'What's this God's name?' What am I supposed to say to them?" God said to Moses, "I Am Who I Am. So, say to the Israelites, 'I Am has sent me to you.'" God continued, "Say to the Israelites, 'The Lord, the God of your ancestors, Abraham's God, Isaac's God, and Jacob's God, has sent me to you.' This is my name forever; this is how all generations will remember me (Exodus 3:11-15).

Then God showed Moses miracles that God would work through him to convince the Israelites the God of their ancestors sent him. God told Moses to throw his staff on the ground, and it turned into a snake and back into a staff. His hand became like leprosy when God told him to put it in his pocket. If the Israelites still didn't believe, God told him, "Take some water from the Nile River and pour it out on dry ground. The water that you take from the Nile will turn into blood on the dry ground." (Exodus 4:9b)

But Moses said to the Lord, "My Lord, I've never been able to speak well, not yesterday, not the day before, and certainly not now since you've been talking to your servant. I have a slow mouth and a thick tongue." Then the Lord said to him, "Who gives people the ability to speak? Who's responsible for making them unable to speak or hard of hearing, sighted or blind? Isn't it I, the Lord? Now go! I'll help you speak, and I'll teach you what you should say." But Moses said, "Please, my Lord, just send someone else."

Then the Lord got angry at Moses and said, "What about your brother Aaron the Levite? I know he can speak very well. He's on his way out to meet you now, and he's looking forward to seeing you. Speak to him and tell him what he's supposed to say. I'll help both of you speak, and I'll teach both of you what to do. Aaron will speak for you to the people. He'll be a spokesperson for you, and you will be like God for him" (Exodus 4:10-16).

Brothers and Sisters in Christ, Moses was scared. He lacked confidence and self-worth. Every time, he pondered upon an excuse, God responded with an answer. Moses felt he wasn't equipped for the mission. However, God equipped him for the journey to complete the mission. Moses' story is all to real for me because I was like Moses! Unfortunately, but fortunately, I understand his pushback and hesitancy. Again, believe it or not, I WAS AN INTROVERT!

My introvert personality used to be atrocious! I would get words jumbled up. Then, I would speak with a babble sometimes. In addition to babbling, I would be anxious and nauseous especially when I had to speak, meet, or sit with unfamiliar people. But this personality slightly surfaced around familiar people too. However, I functioned well in my occupational roles as a teacher, team leader, and facilitator. But put me in a small group with unfamiliar people and I would think about what I wanted to say more than be conversational. It was an eerie feeling. After reading *The Introvert Advantage: How to Thrive in an Extrovert World* by Marti Olsen Laney and *Introvert Power: Why Your Inner Life is Your Hidden Strength* by Laurie Helgow, PhD, I began to understand my inner self. Then I began to use my gifts to advance God's earthly kingdom by thrusting myself into the extrovert world. I'm so enthused that I did because I feel *more* comfortable with writing this book, praying in public, voicing my opinion, making new friends, accepting invitations, posting on social media, and most importantly being God's messenger.

So, I understand Moses's dilemma with obeying God. However, Moses didn't win, and I didn't either. When God calls, you must answer! I've learned God chooses the unexpected least of us to carry out the will of God. In other words, God uses ordinary people to complete extraordinary tasks. With the aforementioned being understood, it was vital for me to realize that all of us have different journeys. As a result, we make it to the finish line at different times in our lives. Additionally, we are created with various gifts and talents to express the love of God and neighbor. Like me, I'm sure you've used Scripture to give you a Christian foundation. I've used many Scripture passages to sustain me in my prophetic journey. My two undergirding scriptures to empower me to defeat the destroyer, when eerie anxious feelings try to seep into my mind are:

"It's impossible for human beings. But all things are possible for God" (Matthew 19:26). From this Scripture, I learned how to trust in the supernatural power of God. In doing so, it helps me to rid myself of thoughts that keep me in the impossible so that I believe in the possibility of God at work on my behalf. In other words, I accept the will of God and believe God will go before me to make my crooked places straight. If I venture into those spaces, God will undergird me with wisdom, strength, and the Holy Spirit will guide me through the curves.

Now, you probably can see why my second Scripture is, "Live by faith and not by sight" (2 Corinthians 5:7). As an introvert, I spent a lot of my life over-processing outcomes. I had determined conclusions before beginning tasks. But when we live by faith and not by sight, we live in the sovereignty of God. We believe God is all powerful and is orchestrating the best for us. Therefore, we can't believe our present burdens will be for a lifetime.

Now you know a little more about my favorite Scriptures. It's time for you to tell me about yourself. Do you have favorite Scriptures to use as weapons for mind wars? If so, what are they? Why are they favorites?

_____

_____

WHO AM I?

I've struggled with this question numerous times. Thus, God always answers me by saying, *You're a prophet of the foretold.* This means God uses me as an earthly vessel to give predicted or futuristic messages to humanity. To help you understand the gifts of prophets, let's look at some of the prophetic messages which foretold about the birth of the Messiah—JESUS.

In the seventh chapter of Isaiah verse 14, the prophet said to the house of David, "Therefore the Lord himself will give you a sign: The virgin will conceive and give birth to a son and will call him Immanuel."

The prophecy was fulfilled with the birth of Jesus. In the Gospel of Matthew, there is a story about Joseph accepting Jesus as his Son. It also entails Isaiah's prophecy. Here is a summary of Joseph accepting Jesus as his Son from the Gospels…

JOSEPH ACCEPTS JESUS AS HIS SON

This is how the birth of Jesus Christ took place. When Mary his mother was engaged to Joseph, before they were married, she became pregnant by the Holy Spirit. Joseph her husband was a righteous man. Because he didn't want to humiliate her, he decided to call off their engagement quietly. As he was thinking about this, an angel from the Lord appeared to him in a dream and said, "Joseph's son of David, don't be afraid to take Mary as your wife, because the child she carries was conceived by the Holy Spirit. She will give birth to a son, and you will call him Jesus, because he will save his people from their sins." Now all of this took place so that what the Lord had spoken through the prophet would be fulfilled:

Look! A virgin will become pregnant and give birth to a son, And they will call him, Emmanuel.
(Emmanuel means "God with us.")

When Joseph woke up, he did just as an angel from God commanded and took Mary as his wife. But he didn't have sexual relations with her until she gave birth to a son. Joseph named him Jesus (Matthew 1:18-25).

This is only one example of a prophet foretelling the birth of the Messiah. There are other prophetic messages foretelling the birth of Jesus. I was going to list them, but I thought just about everyone likes to Google. Therefore, Google to read about prophetic messages in the Bible foretelling the birth of Jesus. You just might discover something new which will deepen your relationship with God. Also, you need to know God's Holy Word for yourself. People can share Old and New Testament stories and favorite Scriptures with you, but there is nothing like reading them on your own.

I must admit that reading to understand the prophetic messages of prophets and to see how their messages were lived out have helped me to understand who I am. Acknowledging who I am always brings tears to my eyes. I guess that's why it has taken me over a year to write this book. When it's published, people will know "Who I Am!" They might ask me how I know I'm a prophet. My response will be, "God told me, and God showed me." If they ask when I came into the realization that I am a prophet, this is some of what I will say:

My prophetic journey began as an adult. I would dream at night about something that I was holding, a place I visited, conversations with people, landmarks, and other life events. Eventually, I would experience the same events of the dream in real time. For example, in my journal in 2009, I began to write about my dreams because I wanted to see the consistency. I also wanted to know how to interpret my dreams. I figured if I wrote about them, I could get them out of my head and onto some paper to analyze and ask God for clarity. Of course, I also wanted more sleep. On January 1, 2009, I have a journey entry in which I wrote: "This has been a good day. I'm a prophet, and I'm understanding who I am. Please allow the Holy Spirit to continue to fall fresh on me. May my latter days be my best days because I would have enjoyed the Holy Spirit."

As I look back at my life now, my latter days are my best days because I know my purpose on earth. What's my purpose on God's earthy kingdom? My purpose is to make disciples of Jesus

Christ so that the world can be transformed. How have I been making disciples? I've accepted my call to shepherd the children of God. Preaching and teaching about the life, death and resurrection of Jesus give me opportunities to make disciples. I teach Jesus welcomes all to his table, and we are forgiven though repentance. Jesus gave his life on the cross so that we may live a new life here on earth by repenting and then work towards sanctifying grace, which means we are working to be more like Jesus Christ. However, we know we'll never be perfect, but we are to keep striving towards perfection. In doing so, we are being shaped more and more into the likeness of Christ by the power of the Holy Spirit.

My other purpose is to deliver messages from God to humanity. This task gets difficult sometimes because I don't want to receive the glory. I want the glory to be given to God. Many times, people get confused by thinking the person who is delivering the message is the one who thoughtfully created the message to be delivered. For that reason, often prophets receive the glory from humanity and not God. But God is the One who gives the message to the prophet. The prophet is the messenger or deliverer.

Nevertheless, I had to learn to use the messages God gave me about my life before I could use them to elevate the spiritual lives of others. Keeping a journal enables me to see how God was working in my life to develop the gifts God has given me.

JOURNAL ENTRIES

I'll share some of my journal with you.

On April 17, 2009, I wrote and acknowledged in my journal entry I'm an evangelist and a prophet of the foretold. After I sat and let those words marinate in my spirit, God told me I would be preaching about the coming of Jesus soon. Then I wrote, "I'm glad I finally realized who I am." I must've thought about what others would think about my calling because my next words in the journal are: "Believe and you will receive whatever you ask for in prayer. Faith comes by hearing and hearing by the word of God. Walk by faith and not by sight, and your paths will be guided. Evangelist of the foretold and many will know."

Beside the last part of this journal entry, I have the word *spirit* underlined several times. Spirit is underlined because I was pondering how was this going to come to be. God told me, *Spirit.* The Holy Spirit transforms me so that I can deliver God's message to others. The spiritual presence of the Trinity—Father, Son, and Holy Spirit—is helping me write this book. As I reflect, my latter days are my best days because I understand the workings of the Holy Spirit. After overcoming my fears, I'm enjoying the presence of the Holy Spirit because I've realized what the Holy Spirit can do through me.

With God's help, I am writing this book about the Second Coming of Jesus. I hope you don't skip to the back, as you may think that is all you need to know. My book builds up to the day Jesus will come and the reasons for His Second Coming. It also tells you a little about myself and my gifts so that you can trust what I have to tell you. I want you to know each chapter builds up to the climatical reason you purchased this book. Also, in some sections I provide lines for reflections. I guess that's the elementary teacher in me who has a desire for us to journey together for understanding and success. In the classrooms, the terminology is called "checks for understanding." As a pastor, I'm using the terminology "reflection."

However, I don't want to take credit, nor be given the glory God deserves, or be put on a pedestal and be perceived as an outcast or a Savior. We have only one Savior and that's Jesus Christ —The Messiah—who gave his life as an atonement for our sins. The truth of the matter is that, if I wasn't constantly being nudge by the Holy Spirit and friends praying for me, this wouldn't be my task. But knowing that I'm working with the "Great I AM" gives me comfort, faith, and trust.

So that you can visualize how God has been working through me like other prophets, I would like to share more of my journal entries and experiences. I've had many journal entries, but the one I would like to share with you is my journal entry on January 24, 2015. God kept telling me I would be ordained. So, I began to wonder if the local pastor route was the one, I should take. If it was, then what was I to do about commissioning and ordination in the United Methodist Church? Then I wrote to God, "You keep telling me to open a daycare. Is that the way to BELIEVE? Then God said, *You'll get a church.*

Please allow me to unpack this for you. You see BELIEVE is a program I've been wanting to implement to support children, youth and adults with study techniques, enrichment classes, secondary education application, setting achievable goals and objectives, as well as teach life skills and Bible study.

As a middle school teacher, my colleague and I implemented an after-school program for students. BELIEVE empowered students to do their best in the classroom, home, and community. Our motto was: If You BELIEVE You Can – You Will. We went on field trips, discussed college entrance exams, study techniques, peer relationships and more. Some of them returned during high school to tell me about their ACT scores and other accomplishments. They were grateful for the after-school program, BELIEVE. When I was appointed to Longstreet United Methodist Church as the lead pastor in May 2015, I implemented an after-school program at the church in September 2018. The name of the program was BELIEVE U CAN! Junior League of Memphis partnered with Longstreet in August 2020 to implement a women's empowerment program to teach life skills. By the time the women's empowerment program began, I was appointed to Collierville United Methodist Church. I was commissioned as a provisional elder at Memphis Annual Conference 2020. With God's help and mentor support, I became an ordained elder at the Tennessee Western Kentucky Annual Conference in June 2023.

God always tells us the truth. But God is still telling me that BELIEVE U CAN will continue to manifest on a much larger scale if I do the work. The program at Longstreet is just a taste of what it can be. So, I guess God is telling me my work isn't done yet. I have more work to do. I receive it, my Lord!!

I chose the name BELIEVE U CAN because I wanted people to empower themselves. After all, these words are empowering me right now to as I write. Let's take a moment to reflect on the words BELIEVE U CAN. How are these words resonating within you?

_____

What aspects of your life do you need to empower yourself?

_____

Will you write an achievable goal to help you accomplish the task of empowering yourself?

_____

Now, let's write three obtainable tasks to assist you with accomplishing your goal. You can call them objectives. Begin them with "I will…

_____

_____

_____

Next, set some time aside and talk to God about your goal and objectives. Make sure you listen. Often when we have our conversations with God, we don't take time to listen. How will we know what to do if we don't listen? Yet don't think you'll receive an immediate answer. I had to learn to listen. Listening gives me epiphanies, and it will do the same for you too. You might get an answer today, the next day, or next day and so on…. Always remember, whenever you receive your answer, God is always right on time. Therefore, don't worry or become anxious. If you do though, I want you to remember Philippians 4:6-7

In your waiting, "Don't be anxious about anything; rather, bring up all of your requests to God in your prayers and petitions, along with giving thanks. Then the peace of God that exceeds all understanding will keep your hearts and minds safe in Christ Jesus." God will give you peace. Just be patient. Trust me. I know from experience.

It is a blessing to be able to have conversations with God, but it's more helpful for us to listen more than we talk to God. If we reminisce on times where we were disappointed because our prayers weren't answered, it was probably because we didn't listen. We become too busy to listen for the answers, chose not to listen, don't know to listen or how to listen. Thus, be rest assured that God will respond or send a tangible response through a person, song, poem, book, etc. You'll get confirmation; therefore, we must patiently wait on God's reply and be at peace in the waiting. I think at times we feel we've prayed and that's it. But being in relationship with God means being in community with God.

As elementary students, we were taught in social studies how communities function. Everyone in the community have individual tasks and these tasks are often the same, similar, or different. People in communities depend on each other by listening to each other's needs and wants. At times, communities function like families who work together for common purposes. In our families and communities, we agree and disagree, but we learn how to love each other through disappointment, pain, joy, love, peace, and happiness. In both units, we have to actively listen and do the same with God. We can't continuously speak over our family and friends and most definitely not God because we'll become mute like Zachariah, who didn't believe in the will of God. His story is told in Luke 1. Feel free to stop and read about him and continue to journey with me later.

As I previously mentioned, God will speak to you. Most of the time, it's a soft, direct yet nurturing voice. It sounds loud because God's voice makes us be still and attentive. Many of you may have learned during your lifetime, loud isn't always heard. Sometimes louder voices parade over softer voices. But it doesn't mean the louder you speak, the more you're heard, or you'll get the tasks completed expeditiously. All voices matter, which is more important than the tone of speech!

The voice of God, our Creator, outweighs all our announces. We depend on God for numerous things on earth. Reciprocally, God depends on us to be the hands and feet of Jesus Christ to carry out God's will. How can we be faithful servants if we don't listen for directions on how to serve?

To help us with our listening journey, God may send people with prophetic voices to give us a message. God knows we're tangible people. Messages from people we can touch and see are more real life to us. Since God is spirit, God works through prophets to help humanity adhere to their call to righteous living. Then, humanity strives to live as Jesus lived by loving God and neighbor—the two Greatest Commandments.

I would like to mention: If humanity wasn't tangible, we wouldn't be passionate about taking care of animals, plants, soil, water, forest, people, and much more! We use our five senses—sight, sound, smell, taste, and touch—to receive sensory information, which allows us to physically and spiritually connect with creation to express our love for creation. Sometimes, we want to express more than agape love, and we begin to sin. The desire to want more and more and more may take us out of a righteous realm with God and lead us into the evil realm of Satan.

But the death and resurrection of Jesus Christ allows us to be redeemed through repentance. Thanks be to God that we can start a new journey with a closer walk with Jesus. Our sins are forgiven through the blood of the Lamb of God, who is Jesus. Do you believe your sins are forgiven through repentance?

CHAPTER TWO

ANOINTING A BLESSING

As a pastor and prophet, I have opportunities to anoint. I began to understand anointing by reading Scripture. In the ninth and tenth chapters of 1 Samuel, there is a story of Saul's anointing. Saul didn't know he was going to be anointed. Samuel didn't know Saul was going to become the king of Israel. But God orchestrated the lost donkeys and the journey of Saul and his servant to the seer, who was the prophet, Samuel. Here's a portion of the story:

> So, Saul and the boy went up to the town, and as they entered it, suddenly Samuel came toward them on his way up to the shrine. Now the day before Saul came, the Lord had revealed the following to Samuel: "About this time tomorrow I will send you a man from the Benjaminite territory. You will anoint him as leader of my people Israel. He will save my people from the Philistines' power because I have seen the suffering of my people, and their cry for help has reached me." When Samuel saw Saul, the Lord told him, "That's the man I told you about. That's the one who will rule my people."
>
> Saul approached Samuel in the city gate and said, "Please tell me where the seer's house is."
>
> "I'm the seer," Samuel told Saul. "Go on ahead of me to the shrine. You can eat with me today. In the morning I'll send you on your way, and I will tell you everything you want to know. As for the donkeys you lost three days ago, don't be worried about

them because they've been found. Who owns all of Israel's treasures, anyway? Isn't it you and your whole family?"

"I'm a Benjaminite," Saul responded, "from the smallest Israelite tribe, and my family is the littlest of the families in the tribe of Benjamin. Why would you say something like that to me?"…Samuel took a small jar of oil and poured it over Saul's head and kissed him. "The Lord hereby anoints you leader of his people Israel," Samuel said. "You will rule the Lord's people and save them from the power of the enemies who surround them. And this will be the sign for you that the Lord has anointed you as leader of his very own possession. When you leave me today, you will meet two men near Rachel's tomb at Zelzah on the border of Benjamin. They will tell you, 'The donkeys you went looking for have been found…And just as Saul turned to leave Samuel's side, God gave him a different heart, and all these signs happened that very same day" (1 Samuel 9 & 10).

Saul was anointed by Samuel as Israel's first king. The Israelites wanted a tangible king instead of a spiritual king. They failed to realize how God delivered them from slavery in Egypt by working through Moses to keep the promises to Abraham, Isaac, and Jacob. Because God loves humanity unconditionally, God answered their request.

You see, prophets have a gift of anointing unlike others. At times, when I anoint in the name of the Father, the Son, and the Holy Spirit, God speaks through me about the person's present and future life experiences. Anointing allows God to work though me so that people can feel the tangible presence of God.

During worship, I've anointed the parishioners with oil and prayed for them. God gives me what to say to them. Many of them mentioned to me that my messages from God was the truth at that moment. Others told me later when the message was revealed to them at a later time. Some thanked me for praying for them. Others walked away in awe or bewilderment. God gave me a message to give to them that was intertwined with what they had been seeking after or struggling with.

In past summers, I anointed the Project Transformation interns who led our eight-week literacy camp on our church campus, Longstreet United Methodist Church. It was an honor to be used by God to give messages about their future, self-identity, and next steps. I asked Nic, who was an intern at Longstreet for several years to share the prophetic message I gave him. I guess I want him to share it so that you will see the validity in my gifts. This sharing isn't for boasting but for understanding. Personally, I had difficulty understanding the validity in my gifts. It wasn't until I saw it in real time and others shared the truth of my prophetic messages to them with me that I realized the authenticity in the gift of my prophetic voice. After all, the Bible tells us to beware of false prophets:

> *Watch out for false prophets. They come to you dressed like sheep, but inside they are vicious wolves. You will know them by their fruit. Do people get bunches of grapes from thorny weeds, or do they get figs from thistles? In the same way, every good tree produces good fruit, and every rotten tree produces bad fruit. A good tree can't produce bad fruit. And a rotten tree can't produce good fruit. Every tree that doesn't produce good fruit is chopped down and thrown into the fire. Therefore, you will know them by their fruit"* (Matthew 7:15-20).

Well, I try to work hard to bear good fruit. Many people can vouch for the genuineness of my character. But, I'm sure there are some people who will say the opposite. Especially the ones who ostracize me for advocating for the Black Lives Matter Movement.

They feel all lives matter and that's what should be advocated. Yes, I agree, but all lives haven't faced over 400 years of oppression. It's not that I'm saying all lives don't matter. I'm saying Black lives matter too. Black lives have not been treated humanely for four centuries. We have depended upon God, songs, writings, quotes, and Black icons to help us persevere through our obstacles and to give us hope.

Throughout my life, I have learned words matter. Words can tear people to pieces and make them become like shredded paper that is discarded in the trashcan. Words hurt and can make people lose confidence, self-worth, and their outlook on life. On the other hand, words can give people wings like an eagle to help them soar from the depth of valleys to get to clear blue skies. The soaring allows people to gain confidence and have a positive outlook on life. They feel obstacles are means to growth instead of stifling growth.

Thus, words can make us feel **worthy** or **worthless.**

As a prophet who gets words from God to deliver to God's children, every word of God is exceptional, trustworthy, honest, and valid. Sometimes we may not want to hear the uncomfortable truth; therefore, we rebel. However, there is validity in discomfort. We must always remember the word of God is a lamp unto our feet and a light for our paths. At a Project

Transformation banquet, Nicholas shared how his path was illuminated by a prophetic message. Before I share his message with you, I would like to tell you Project Transformation (PT) is an eight-week summer literacy camp for rising first through sixth graders. College interns lead the camp and churches volunteer to read one on one with children. The college interns engage in activities that lead to spiritual growth. The church connects to its community. College students connect with children. It's a win-win-win opportunity in being the hands and feet of Christ.

Here's a portion of Nicolas's witness statement. Again, I'm only sharing it with you so that you can gain confidence in who God has called me to be—a prophet of the foretold.

One night, toward the end of the summer, our intern community found ourselves in a late-night conversation. These were always my favorite. We do not really talk about our faith at school. But PT provided a safe space where we can sit around and explore faith together. That night, our conversations focused on the fears we had for the next part of our journey after we left Project Transformation. I shared for the first time that I was considering becoming a teacher. Another intern shared she was considering pursuing a theology degree. She knew she had a passion for it, and she was trying to figure out what that meant. I remember her saying that she hadn't shared this with anyone else—we were the first people to know.

A few days later, we were at our final Sunday morning worship with our site church. Pastor Tondala invited our intern team to stand, and each received a blessing as we concluded our summer internship. Pastor Tondala began to pray over us—one by one. She came to me and said, "I know there is something you want to do, but you're struggling. God is telling me to tell you to take the risk, follow your passion. God will be there for you."

"Hmmm," I wondered. "Is this about teaching?"

She moved to the next intern—my friend who had shared the night before. "God is telling me that you have a strong passion for theology," Pastor Tondala told her. "Don't let anything hold you back."

My friend began to cry. Pretty soon, we were all in tears. That was the first time I really experienced the Holy Spirit. I knew the Lord was speaking to me through Pastor Tondala.

After that, I returned to school and added an education certificate to my major. I want to be a physics teacher someday. Wow, just saying that makes me happy. As soon as I made that decision, I found that I was no longer a wandering physics major. I had purpose. I wasn't just learning physics to learn physics. Now, I knew what I wanted to do with it. I was learning physics because I wanted to be able to teach it to my students. I want to be a good teacher, and so I need to learn the content for my students. All of the sudden, I began to enjoy what I was learning. And my grades reflected that... No more Cs. Today, my fellow classmates look to me as a leader.

Nicholas is an awesome leader! Sometimes we just need to hear from others so that our gifts and talents within us spring out of us. The campers at PT loved him. Every day he had a huddle of children around him, while he taught them the importance of making Christ-like choices. Of course, it was probably some of the same lessons their parents told them. But for some reason, hearing it from college student leaders gave campers an opportunity to see how leadership roles evolves from being children, youth, young adults, and then older adults. The four-day, eight week, 9 am to 3 pm relationship aided the campers in seeing their leadership potential because the interns were closer to their age than their parents. Nicholas was a faithful PT leader. He soared like an eagle. To be honest, I didn't know my gift of prophecy helped him to discern his career path. After all, I was saying what God wanted me to say. But I've learned when prophets give messages to others from God, it is what the recipient needed to hear at that time. Nicholas was a struggling physics major in college. He knew he liked physics, but he wasn't quite sure where it would take him. Therefore, he was praying and seeking direction. God answered his prayers by giving him direction. I'm just thankful to have been part of God's plan to give him clarity. *Thanks be to God!*

At the time I began writing this book, I was at Longstreet. I asked a parishioner to write something about my prophetic voice. Lynn Rawlings wrote:

The first thing I noticed about Pastor Tondala was her beautiful infectious smile. Then she began to preach. Oh, my heavens, it was wonderful! You could feel that the Holy Spirit was in her and leading her to say what God wanted her to say. Sometimes it was hard because she would hesitate just a second before saying whatever God wants her to say. But she always continued, and it was something I needed to hear.

One Sunday God told her to give everyone a blessing, a personal blessing. So, we all got up and went to where she stood to receive "our" blessing. She told us things only the Holy Spirit and God knew about us. She prayed for each one of us individually and I knew it was from God and the Holy Spirit. In the time she has been here, she has grown in every way. She has also helped me to grow. I'm so glad God brought her to Longstreet and to me.

To be honest, I really didn't know I had such an impact on Lynn and my other members until we were in conversation about my gifts. I was talking to her about her gift of cooking because it's certainly not my gift! I have a few things that I can cook, but I'm not a master chef. However, both of us talked about how God created us with different gifts to exercise our dominion on earth. The book of Genesis affirms the necessity for us to use our gifts so that the world can function. Genesis 1:26-28 states:

> *Then God said, "Let us make humankind in our image, according to our likeness; and let them have dominion over the fish of the sea, and over the birds of the air, and over the cattle, and over all the wild animals of the earth and over every creeping thing that creeps upon the earth." So God created humankind in his image, in the image of God he created them; male and female he created them. God blessed them, and God said to them, "Be fruitful and multiply, and fill the earth and subdue it; and have dominion over the fish of the sea and over the birds of the air and over every living thing that moves upon the earth.*

In the creation story, God gave humanity dominion to take care of the world God created. Sometimes, I think we need educating on the word *dominion*. So, let's take this time to do that—after all I'm a licensed elementary teacher too. I think I'm qualified for a vocabulary lesson. *Dominion* means to have charge of something when you are ruling over it. Therefore, God has given us the charge to rule over creation. Unfortunately, people have used the word to exercise oppression of humanity instead of nurturing humanity. This evolved traction of the word happens when we think we know what's best for others. Also, when we begin to think that we know what's best for others, we expect others to lose themselves so that we can assimilate them in a particular culture. But who's to say which culture is correct. After all, my ancestors were assimilated into the melting pot of European culture. For that reason, I know very little about my African heritage or way of life. But I do know about the European way of life and what I need to accomplish to be successful. Although having a prophetic voice wasn't on my balance beam of accomplishments; however, I am thankful for my gift from God. I have realized that it's okay to be different. Accepting our differences allows us to embrace who God created us to be. When we understand that, it is then that we can use our free will to build up the kingdom of God with God's plans as our guide and not our own. Therefore, as a true disciple of Jesus Christ, we become less concerned about pleasing humanity and more concerned about being faithful at serving our Creator—God.

To tell you the truth, I was nervous when Nicholas told his story. At the banquet, I shrunk in my seat because everyone present at the Project Transformation banquet were aware of my gifts. I thought they would tell others; therefore, my secret would be OUT! I didn't believe it was out before but releasing it was my choice, not theirs. All the sudden, I felt like I had lost control over who I want to know about my prophetic gifts from God. However, after some soul-searching reflections to calm my anxiety, I realized it was the best thing that could've happened to me. Now, I have an expanded support system of people who trusts the calling God has given me, which is to free the oppressed by bringing them Good News from our Heavenly Father.

CHAPTER THREE

HOW DID I GET HERE?

How did I get here to write this book is a question I've asked myself over and over and over. The only answer I get from God is, *You have to be obedient.* I must admit that I have procrastinated on writing this book. I guess I really don't want people to think I possess magical powers. Well, I must tell you being obedient to God will get us out of our comfort zone.

God will send us to places we never thought we will go to. When I accepted my pastoral call, I thought I would be appointed to African American United Methodist Churches. But as I'm writing this book, I'm at my second cross-racial appointment. In other words, this is my second time pastoring a predominately Caucasian congregation. Both appointments have given me opportunities to grow in being comfortable in the skin that God created me to live in. As a pastor, I've grown in accepting people as they are and offering grace whenever needed. Spiritual growth intertwined with learning the culture of different ethnicities is an ongoing adventure.

Speaking of growth, I guess I'm still growing now. Every time I'm afraid or hesitate at doing the will of God, God always whispers to me, *I have called you by name. You are my Beloved Daughter whom I have selected to bring Good News to everyone.*

When I realized that I was the one to bring the Good News about the Second Coming, I was in shock. And yet, I felt highly favored in the Lord as well. I guess I had a Mary, the mother of Jesus moment, like when the angel Gabriel visited her to tell her she would give birth to Jesus. I need to tell you that I am surprised my Lord wants to use me in this way. I'm just shocked! I've procrastinated because maybe I'm not the one to share this message. However, I guess I am because I keep getting nudges. Furthermore, I'm not getting any peace until I finish this journal. As I'm writing this, I understand why Mary felt highly favored. Thus, I'm not like Mary at all because she didn't procrastinate on her reply nor her actions. I don't know how she could have procrastinated on being pregnant by the Holy Spirit anyway. Yet, both of us had questions, and they were answered. Here's Mary's story in the Gospel of Luke chapter 1:

> ....*When Elizabeth was six months pregnant, God sent the angel Gabriel to Nazareth, a city in Galilee, to a virgin who was engaged to a man named Joseph, a descendant of David's house. The virgin's name was Mary. When the angel came to her, he said, "Rejoice, favored one! The Lord is with you!" She was confused by these words and wondered what kind of greeting this might be. The angel said, "Don't be afraid, Mary. God is honoring you. Look! You will conceive and give birth to a son, and you will name him Jesus. He will be great and he will be called the Son of the Most High. The Lord God will give him the throne of David his father. He will rule over Jacob's house forever, and there will be no end to his kingdom."*
>
> *Then Mary said to the angel, "How will this happen since I haven't had sexual relations with a man?"*
>
> *The angel replied, "The Holy Spirit will come over you and the power of the Most High will overshadow you. Therefore, the one who is to be born will be holy. He will be called God's Son. Look, even in her old age, your relative Elizabeth has conceived a son. This woman who was labeled 'unable to conceive' is now six months pregnant. Nothing is impossible for God."*
>
> *Then Mary said, "I am the Lord's servant. Let it be with me just as you have said." Then the angel left her.*

I'm sure Mary didn't wake up and say to herself, "I am going to give birth to the long-awaited Messiah. His name will be Jesus, and he will save the world from their sins through repentance." Instead, she was surprised yet grateful and willing to serve God in a supernatural way. I would have to say that I didn't think I would be waking up early in the morning to write about the Second Coming of Jesus. Consequently, I'm thankful God finds me worthy to do the task.

The only forethought I had about the Second Coming was when I watched *I, ROBOT.*

This vision encircled my life in 2017. For those who have no clue of what I'm talking about, I'll give you a synopsis of the movie as well as why I chose to watch it on a particular day.

I love action movies! On the weekends, I always find myself folding clothes or cleaning up to my favorite TV show or movie. At times the family room, kitchen, and bedroom televisions are on the same channel to make sure I don't miss a moment while cleaning. I'm thankful I can rewind to the scene I missed while I'm walking to another room, taking out the trash or cleaning the bathrooms. I can truly say the DVR feature from DIRECTV is awesome!

But when I find an intriguing movie, I fold clothes. It seems like laundry becomes purposeful when I'm folding clothes while watching movies. I stop bouncing from room to room to lounge in the moment of excitement while completing my laundry duties. Of course, I can rewind to view missed scenes, but I don't want to interrupt the flow of the movie. Sometimes, I'll input the captions to make sure I understand every word. And when my husband comes into my space to talk to me, I take a deep breath and pause the movie. During our conversation, I'm eagerly waiting for him to finish so that I can continue the movie and bask in enthrallment. When he's watching sports, these feelings are reciprocal. By the way, interruptions are when I use the DVR feature.

Am I the only one who does this?

Anyway, *I, ROBOT is* the movie with Will Smith portraying a police officer. The Saturday I chose to watch *I,ROBOT* was when I refused to *watch Law & Order: Special Victims Unit*. I had seen that particular episode several times. You know, I'll watch the same episode two times but watching three or four of the same episodes of any *Law & Order* is overwhelming to me. But that's not how I feel about all movies because I'm a *Black Panther* fanatic and *Home Alone* makes me burst in tears of laughter repeatedly.

But since I didn't want to watch repeats of my favorite crime show, I started searching Netflix. As I was scrolling, I saw *I,ROBOT* with Will Smith. I told myself, *I haven't watched this before. Will Smith always makes good movies!* After reading the description, I decided to give it a try. Here's a synopsis of the movie in case you have no idea of the movie I'm referring to or you need a refresher:

Will Smith portrays the character of a police officer who nearly drowned. He is saved by a robot and given a robotic lung and arm. His near-death drowning experience makes him detests robots. Why? Because the robot saves him from drowning rather than a little girl who was drowning. The robot saves Will because his chance of survival is greater according to the robot's calculations. The storyline for this movie is in the year of 2035. Will Smith plays Detective Spooner, who is curious to the reason why U.S. Robotics founder Dr. Alfred Lanning played by James Cromwell dies. Spooner believes there is more to the presumed suicidal death of the professor. He solves the case, with the assistance of Dr. Susan Calvin, who is actress Bridget Moynahan. I like watching her on *Blue Bloods* by the way.

The movie was fascinating. Yet, it left me bewildered, so I began to ponder. I was astonished at the development of future technology. While pondering, I became appalled with the role replacement of humanity that was given to robots. I immediately thought of the cartoon, *The Jetsons*. This animated cartoon by Hanna Barbara has a household maid robot named Rosie for the Jetson family. Rosie loves the Jetson Family. She completed chores and had a few flaws; however, Rosie had human emotions like Sonny on *I, ROBOT*.

In *I, ROBOT*, the robots are assigned to obey three laws which are: protect humans, obey humans, and protect themselves. However, the laws begin to conflict with each other and VIKI dives into an unaccepted protection mode for humanity. This 2004 science fiction movie is worth watching.

Now, I have to admit that God didn't say robots were going to destroy humanity. But we do need to understand the ramifications of the obligations we give to them. Humanoid robots replacing the daily chores of humanity will confine humanity to live out less of our own lives. I guess you're wondering how could that be? Because we would love for a robot to do household chores. You're probably thinking, *What are you complaining about? If you had a robot to do your chores, you could relax and watch as much television as you like without having to rewind or turn on your favorite shows throughout the house while you're cleaning.… What's the issue, Tondala?*

The wailing issue is that I believe sometimes we fail to understand the need to develop relationships with our family. We strive to develop relationships with friends, but in most families, relationships are responsibility centered. I agree to the fact that each family member has a role in their family unit to make it function as a whole. But, it's necessary for families to exert their individual well-being by being in vital conversations with each other about their own life experiences to build togetherness.

For instance, let's talk about how the house chore of washing dishes evolved in my house. My husband, Alan, and I are empty nesters. We use the dishwasher a lot now. In the past when our sons, Justin and Jeremy, were at home, we washed the dishes by hand to demonstrate the art of dishwashing. When they were old enough, we washed the dishes together until they were capable to wash them on their own. Unfortunately, I believe I missed the step of teaching them to wipe the stove and sweep the floor. To help them along, I swept the floor and wiped the appliances that night or the next day. I would tell them wiping the stove, refrigerator, and counter, cleaning the sink, and sweeping the floor are included in cleaning the kitchen, but they didn't do it consistently. Therefore, it didn't get done consistently. I should've switched roles or allowed them to clean the entire kitchen. Well, it's too late now, and I hope they've learned how to clean the entire kitchen.

During the time I taught them to wash dishes, we talked about different kinds of dish detergent— how the inexpensive dish detergent doesn't keep your dish water soapy or clean greasy dishes well and how to use scrubbing pads to remove stuck on food. If I didn't ask them about their school day when they arrived home or at dinner, we discussed it during dishwashing or later that night. I have to admit: dishwashing wasn't done by them nightly, but I inquired about their day just about every day.

Since I'm not a handy woman, my husband taught them maintenance skills. He also cooked, and we cleaned the kitchen. Speaking of cooking, I quickly learned the difference between cooking and baking. I have a passion for baking but not cooking. Recently, my sons told other family members at dinner, "Momma cooked the fun foods like breakfast, tacos, hamburgers, and Hamburger Helper. Daddy cooked the soul foods like fried chicken, beans, spaghetti, and BBQ." Well, I would like to say that I've learned to cook a few soul food dishes now like lasagna. My family loves my lasagna. I can also cook greens and pinto beans. Salisbury steaks, mashed potatoes, green beans, and biscuits is one of their favorite meals. Of course, the green beans are canned and the biscuits are the frozen ones that you put in the oven. Hey, I'm not a chef, but I've mastered cooking a few more dishes throughout the years, and I'm thankful. However, I still love baking, and my husband cooks dinner during the week and Saturday morning breakfast. I clean the kitchen. Some things just don't change over the years. I'm beyond grateful!

How about your household? Do you cook, bake or both? Who cleans the kitchen?

_____

_____

Again, my husband taught our sons maintenance skills such as changing the oil in vehicles and replacing lights, wipers, brakes along with using lawn equipment and much more. He talked to them about life experiences. Completing household tasks and having vital conversations to promote togetherness allowed us to take ownership of our responsibilities, which gave us a sense of purpose. It diversified our skills, helped with character formation, and opened the door for necessary conversations. We aren't a perfect family because we aren't perfect people. But we love each other and express our love in different ways. How are you expressing your love to your family?

_____

_____

In our family, Alan and I discussed conflict resolution strategies with our sons and how to meet and greet people with a firm handshake and eye contact. As adults they are sociable, but they still love their peace and quiet like their parents.

Even though we love serene moments, we also love family and friend gatherings. These gatherings are essential because we learn how to solve conflict peacefully, have cross cultural conversations, and develop reasonable short- and long-term relationships. In the gathering spaces, we can begin to understand the concept of meeting people where they are and learn how our similarities and differences make us unique. Since God can't do the work alone in building up the Kingdom of God on earth, we understand each of us has a role. The Holy Spirit equips humanity to do the will of God. I have to ask the question: How will the Holy Spirit equip robots to do God's will? The Holy Spirit works through humanity, and we can't program the Holy Spirit.

In Acts 2:1-21, there is a story about the apostles receiving the Holy Spirit. Let's take a look.

> *When the day of Pentecost came, they were all together in one place. Suddenly a sound like the blowing of a violent wind came from heaven and filled the whole house where they were sitting. They saw what seemed to be tongues of fire that separated and came to rest on each of them. All of them were filled with the Holy Spirit and began to speak in other tongues as the Spirit enabled them.*

> *Now there were staying in Jerusalem God-fearing Jews from every nation under heaven. When they heard this sound, a crowd came together in bewilderment, because each one heard their own language being spoken. Utterly amazed, they*

asked: "Aren't all these who are speaking Galileans? Then how is it that each of us hears them in our native language? Parthians, Medes and Elamites; residents of Mesopotamia, Judea and Cappadocia, Pontus and Asia, Phrygia and Pamphylia, Egypt and the parts of Libya near Cyrene; visitors from Rome (both Jews and converts to Judaism); Cretans and Arabs—we hear them declaring the wonders of God in our own tongues!" Amazed and perplexed, they asked one another, "What does this mean?"

Some, however, made fun of them and said, "They have had too much wine."

Then Peter stood up with the Eleven, raised his voice and addressed the crowd: "Fellow Jews and all of you who live in Jerusalem, let me explain this to you; listen carefully to what I say. These people are not drunk, as you suppose. It's only nine in the morning!"

No, this is what was spoken by the prophet Joel:
"'In the last days, God says,
I will pour out my Spirit on all people.
Your sons and daughters will prophesy,
your young men will see visions,
your old men will dream dreams.
Even on my servants, both men and women,
I will pour out my Spirit in those days,
and they will prophesy.

I will show wonders in the heavens above
and signs on the earth below,
blood and fire and billows of smoke.
The sun will be turned to darkness
and the moon to blood
before the coming of the great and glorious day of the Lord.
And everyone who calls
on the name of the Lord will be saved."

Do you know the Holy Spirit guides and equips us for righteous behavior? We become better people because of the transformation that happens in us with the third person of the Godhead, which is the Holy Spirit. The transformation happens because of the change in our hearts. Loving God and Loving Neighbor become our priorities. We seek ways to live out our purpose in life by being the hands and feet of Jesus Christ. Our Savior Jesus Christ went against normal Jewish society behaviors. Hanging out with tax collectors, engaging in conversation with the Samaritan woman at the well, healing the outcasts, allowing women to follow him are a few examples of Jesus being inclusive not exclusive. Jesus' actions let us know all are welcome to the Kingdom of God. We just need to accept the invitation, which was given to us before we knew anything about the Trinity—God the **Father**, God's **Son** Jesus, and the **Holy Spirit.**

Methodist founder, John Wesley, calls this unknown invitation Prevenient Grace. Grace is the love and mercy given to us by God because God wants us to have it, not because of anything we have done to deserve it. It is the free gift of God, which is stated in Ephesians 2:8-9: *"For by grace you have been saved through faith, and this is not our own doing, it is the gift of God – not the result of works, so that no one may boast."* Prevenient Grace is the love of God wooing us. The will of God draws us closer by pursuing us, freeing us, and empowering us. We don't know that it's God, but our sovereign God knows. Because God actively seeks us, we do not have to beg and plead for God's love and grace. God's Prevenient Grace causes us to want to develop a relationship with God. It enables us to discern the difference between good and evil, which makes it possible for us to choose good. When we understand that difference, we experience God's justifying grace as we can receive God's unconditional love for us. We know in our hearts that Jesus died on the cross for our sins. We believe our sins are forgiven and we are made just with God. As we strive to live as Jesus lived but know we will never be perfect, we experience sanctifying grace. All of us are children of God, and God expresses love to us all. We need God's grace and grace from others.

I believe God's grace is sufficient for us. God's power is made perfect in our weakness so that we can become the person God created us to be. Through Christ's death on the cross, we are justified. We are offered the opportunity of salvation. Thus, we are expected to live and grow in the likeness of Christ. Since we live in an evil world and saved by God's grace and mercy, divine grace allows us to be in-tuned with Christ's love. This enables us to be forgiving like Joseph, whose brothers sold him into slavery out of jealousy. Most importantly, Sanctifying Grace helps us to continue our journey of Christian perfection. Since Jesus was physically on earth, we are given the opportunity to spiritually and physically be the hands and feet of Christ. We begin this journey with Prevenient Grace and the Holy Spirit works within us to transform us into Christlike people.

I have to admit that I didn't fully understand the work of the Holy Spirit as I was raising my children. I'm not ashamed; however, I'm grateful for clarity. Now, I can honestly share with family, friends, congregations, strangers, and more the work of the Holy Spirit from my experiences.

What do you understand about the Holy Spirit?

_____

_____

CHAPTER FOUR

CLAP YOUR HANDS WITH THANKSGIVING FOR TECHNOLOGY

I believe all of us are thankful for the advancement of household appliances. Let's clap, clap, clap, clap for technology. Of course, a dishwasher to expedite the chore of dishwashing instead of a pail allocates more time for other activities. A washer to keep your knuckles from being bruised from a clothes-washing board is a must have. A refrigerator and stove to store and cook hearty meals without dry ice, wood, and coals are essential in the twenty-first century. Living like the animated cave family, the Flintstones, would be challenging for me and maybe you too. My feet aren't big enough to hit the pavement to drive me around. Because dinosaurs are extinct, they can't assist humanity with labor anymore. Construction machinery also known as oversized Tonka Trucks have replaced the labor of dinosaurs, and humanity is being replaced by artificial intelligence.

Thus, I'm afraid advances in technology will lessen humanity's existence and keep us distant from each other. Cellular phones are keeping us from engaging in fruitful conversations at home, restaurants, checkout lines, breaks, and lunches at work and school. Toddlers have tablets and phones too. Don't get me wrong: we need our phones, and toddlers need to be safely occupied. But, cell phones shouldn't replace valuable conversing and nurturing.

So, let's talk about the advancement of technology? The viral pandemic called Coronavirus also known as COVID-19 flipped the world upside down. We're still experiencing its ramifications.

But there will come a time when the virus will be less prevalent as it is now. Scientists will continue to engage in extensive research to discuss the virus in present and future. Therefore, I'm just going to take some time to talk about recent history, since this journal will become your family's heirloom.

In 2019 as people were becoming infected with COVID, the world began to mourn. We didn't know what was going on because this virus is much different from the flu even though you may experience flu-like symptoms. As the death toll increased, people prepared for services of remembrance. At first, Celebration of Life services were attended in great numbers; however, as the COVID cases increased attendance declined. People couldn't come and celebrate the life of their family members and friends, which made them grieve more. Those in attendance had to wear masks and affectionate hugs were at the bare minimum.

The virus seems to be more detrimental to communities of color because of inadequate healthcare, distrust in the validity of the government, and underlying health conditions such as diabetes, heart, and lung disease as well as high blood pressure. I can recall when COVID-19 began, people were saying the virus wouldn't affect people of color. Fortunately, Black and Brown movie and sport celebrities felt compelled to post on social media and televise events to speak against this false belief. Celebrities of different ethnicities, who contracted the virus, posted on social media platforms to let everyone know COVID-19 isn't exclusive but inclusive. It doesn't skip over communities of color. Sometimes people are asymptomatic, or they may experience shortness of breath, rapid heartbeat, congestion, cough, fatigue, and muscle aches. Symptoms vary from person to person. However, if you have underlying conditions relating to heart, lung, or diabetes, COVID-19 can be life threatening. The virus intensifies diagnosed and undiagnosed illnesses.

My church conference, the legacy United Methodist Memphis Conference, hosted the Black Methodist for Church Renewal "Ask the Docs" panel discussion so that churches would know how to plan for worship. Also, hearing the truth from real time Methodist LeBonheur Healthcare Chief Medical Officers gave clarity to a world pandemic. Taking part in the programming allowed others to see that I believe and trust the facts, which was essential being that the world was and still is being wounded by the pandemic of COVID-19.

When I became infected with the Coronavirus in December 2020, I prayed for God to heal me on earth because a small percentage of people died from the virus without underlying conditions. I didn't want to be in the mortality percentage in this global pandemic; however, I had accepted the fact that I was in the infected percentage. Accepting that reality was overwhelming. When I tested negative, I sent a video to family and friends. I didn't post it on social media, since my friends, associates, and church members died from COVID-19. I didn't want to make it seem as though I was gloating and being inconsiderate even though I felt grateful and considerate.

When the pandemic reached its heights, a paradigm shift happened. States mandated "Safer at Home" policies. Restaurants, companies, organizations, schools, gyms, churches, etc. closed to isolate the spread of the virus. Only essential workers were allowed to travel, and, of course, essential businesses remained opened. To stay connected to a community, people of all generations began to use more social media to communicate with family and friends.

We had the luxury of enjoying free concerts by various artists, who just wanted to ease the pain, tension, and grief in our secluded world. Personal trainers journeyed to rooftops to get people up and moving by giving training lessons without cost or membership. All you had to do was have a willing spirit to exercise on your balcony or with widows open. Waves and loving kisses were felt through windows and plexiglass at nursing homes and the homes of grandchildren, grandparents, parents, and other places where people wanted to put their eyes on their loved ones and prison-touch them as well. Graduations, baby showers, birthdays, wedding showers, and a host of other celebrations were remembered with drive-by gatherings. Yard signs brought awareness to celebrations.

Since people couldn't attend in-person worship at churches, virtual worship attendance began to increase. For some, it was an easy transition because they already had a virtual audience; therefore, they transitioned to virtual only. Others had to figure out how to do virtual worship, and some churches didn't join the virtual world. The non-virtual church connected with each other with newsletters and weekly mailed sermons.

I was appointed to Longstreet, when COVID-19 introduced itself to the world. At Longstreet when the "Safer at Home" mandate began, we worshipped by way of conference call. Later the Memphis Conference of the United Methodist Church offered grants for Zoom. I applied and received a grant, which allowed us to worship by way of conference call and Zoom. Because of the desire of most of my congregation not wanting to connect to the digital world for church, we had more conference-call worshippers.

I believe society is thankful for technology, and I am too. Social media platforms like Facebook, Google Meet, TicToc, Instagram, Twitter, YouTube, and others soothed our hearts and minds because we can communicate with family, friends, coworkers, and carry out business administration. Humanity is thankful for those who created these platforms because social media gives us a sense of community during this pandemic. They also give churches avenues to share the Good News.

When churches opened, worshippers masked up. By this time, I was appointed to Collierville United Methodist Church. We adhered to the social distance 6-ft protocol and disinfected continuously, according to the guidelines of the Center for Disease Control (CDC) and local health departments. I would have to say it was challenging to withdraw from embracing church members and guests. We had become acclimated to welcome people with handshakes, hugs, and pats on the shoulder to display compassion, acceptance, and appreciation of our Brothers and Sisters in Christ. But air hugs, fist bumps, winks, waves, and other gestures sustained us when we were deep in the valleys of the pandemic.

Since the vaccine rollout and real time CDC guidelines, we've become more relaxed with masks, embraces, and face-to-face conversations in church, work, school, stores, and other places. However, at times, I still fist and elbow bump those who are wearing masks because greeting is at one's own comfort level. We don't know when the world will be pandemic free of the Coronavirus. The virus might linger around and surface time and time again like the flu.

As you may know, there is still some hesitancy about taking the COVID vaccination, since it was developed at warp speed. Advances in technology and scientists collaborating played major roles in the amount of time it took to develop COVID vaccines. My husband and I took the Pfizer vaccine and got boosted before Christmas 2021. We got another booster summer 2022. For all injections, we went together for support and unity. Plus, this is a historical moment; therefore, we wanted to venture together. One day, we expect to tell our grandkids about our journey, when they read about the Coronavirus in history books.

Currently, COVID-19 is still taking us on roller coaster rides with its low to high infection rates. Thus, we must continue to believe God is with us and God will never leave or forsake us!

Do you believe God is with us? How do you know?

_____

_____

Also, what are your thoughts about technology? Do you believe technology is for humanity or against humanity?

_____

_____

With me giving accolades about technology and then questioning its advances, you may think I dislike technological advancements. I don't, and God doesn't either. However, God wants humanity to use our gifts and graces so that our skills won't diminish. Of course, technology has captivated humanity in many facets. People from all generations are using it. Toddlers and children are learning how to turn on their tablets to view their favorite shows. Youth are watching less of their favorite television shows on flat screens because they can tune in to them on their cellular phones or maneuver their favorite apps. My granddaughters, Kyla and Aaliyah, watch Netflix on their phones, which makes me ponder about the usage of televisions and satellite services in future centuries. Older adults who are struggling with getting to know their Samsung or iPhone ask the younger generation for…. HELP! Or they watch instructional videos.

Additionally, most instruction manuals for devices, appliances, and equipment are available online instead of being readily accessible to purchasers. I'm sure the reason is to decrease printing costs to keep products affordable. But, I also believe a remnant of people would appreciate the return of printed instructional manuals with new products. What's your opinion about saving trees to lessen consumer cost but yet having to go online or watch a video for instructions?

_____

I've had dual feelings regarding this topic, which means that I can have a written or an online copy, and I will be content. But I do have a file in my cabinet labeled manuals. I guess I need to check to see if they can be discarded especially if I don't own the item anymore or its online. I guess it's time to purge the file cabinet.

But let's get back to what began the advanced technology or artificial intelligence reflections. Remember, it was the movie I, ROBOT. After watching the movie, I began to reflect on how humanity began to depend on robots to complete their daily life tasks. In other words, robots began to be created to take on the domestic and parenting responsibilities of the lives of humanity. Have you ever thought whether or not robots should be used to complete household chores? For instance, sweeping, washing dishes, vacuuming, feeding pets, laundry, preparing meals, cleaning bathrooms, dusting, etc.?

_____

Also, should robots be given the responsibility to nurture babies, children, and teens? Should the nurturing life changing moments of feeding, dependency, self-worth, and guidance be given to steel instead of flesh? Should a robot's sensor receive and control emotions instead of a human's loving heart? I just asked some thought-provoking questions. Feel free to take your time to answer.

_____

_____

_____

Proverbs 22:6 tells us, *"Train children in the way they should go; when they grow old, they won't depart from it."* It doesn't say to train up a robot in the way he should go and when he is old replace it. Parenting children fosters opportunities for them to understand how to live a righteous life and have healthy relationships with themselves, family, friends, associates, and God.

I believe we know; there is a major difference between someone controlling your actions instead of you being in control of your own actions. Additionally, I believe there is value in human relationships with each other. In my relationships, I've learned how to express emotions as well as how to become more confident in my life roles as a mother, wife, pastor, disciple, friend, cousin, aunt, sister, and so on. These roles allow me to enjoy the impactful and loving gift of human relationships.

Why am I mentioning these things? God told me too. After all, I'm a prophet of the foretold. In the vast future, robots will become a household member, be used extensively for military combat, and continue to replace occupations that were once occupied by humanity. When I foresee the futuristic uses for robots, I become mortified. Numerous questions come to my mind. Let's see what you think about my analyzation.

Regarding robots being household members, concerns are surfacing in my mind. Since they are depended upon human controllers for functioning to have them in the household adds to tasks.

Even though the robot is replacing domestic tasks to make family life easier, their presence is very questionable. Will human reproduction decrease to support the cost for robotic purchase, repairs, and upgrades? What are your thoughts?

_____

Parents know the cost of raising one child is astronomical. Imagine if you have more than one with no hand-me-down clothes, toys, furniture, and other necessities. From birth to high school graduation and adding secondary education can nearly empty your wallets or max out your credit cards especially if parents didn't financially prepare for your child's future. Then there's marriage with wedding plans and lots of giving. Sometimes our children experience a financial crisis and need our assistance in their adulting journey. You see, high school graduation shouldn't cease the nurturing we give to our children, grandchildren, and others. If you're thinking, *It sounds like Tondala is reflecting on experience,* then you're correct. What about you?

_____

During my meditation time, I couldn't help but ponder on the question: Will robots out reproduce humanity because of cost and the need to do less? Of course, some of you will say working less means more time for romance, but robotic maintenance won't be cheap. I don't know the cost, but I do know that technical repair fees can become expensive. As a result, the maintenance is likely to replace the cost of a child. For instance, a family who initially planned on raising four children might be more prone to have three heirs because the robot will be the fourth domesticated helper.

Thus, the question remains: Will humanoid robots out produce humanity because of cost and the need of humanity to work less?

_____

Again, Proverbs 22:6 tell us to, *"Train children in the way they should go; when they grow old, they won't depart from it."* The verse doesn't say train up a robot in the way they should go, when they grow old do more maintenance or replace it so they won't leave you without a helper.

To be honest, I thought it was absurd to think humanoid robots and other artificial intelligence could take the place of humanity's life experiences. But once I began to ponder on the occupations that have already been somewhat substituted for humans, it becomes all too real.

Let's gander and reflect on some of these occupations. Write your thoughts about how you noticed humans are being replaced by artificial intelligence. I believe this legalized replacement should be called 'The Human Replacement Theory. If you need to Google for further research and to resonate your thoughts, feel free to do so. If your thoughtful conclusion doesn't resonate with mine, express it on the lines too.

• Assembly-line and factory workers

_____

• Self-driving cars

_____

• Telephone operators

_____

• Cashiers

_____

• Stockers

_____

• Pharmacist and Pharmacy Technicians

_____

• Pilots

_____

• Military Combat

_____

- Postal Workers

_____

- Surgeons

_____

- Travel Agents

_____

- Switchboard Operators

_____

_____

Do you have others to list?

_____

_____

_____

As you have read and analyzed how robots and computers are replacing occupations in which humans worked to earn a living, what are your final thoughts and conclusions? _____

_____

_____

Over the years, I watch sanitation workers release a mechanical arm to pick up the trash and dump it in the truck. In the past, most sanitation workers would walk to the curb, get the trash, and take it to the dump truck. Of course, the mechanical arm is more sanitary, safer, and requires far less effort; however, residents had opportunities to greet and become more sociable with essential workers. Relationships were intentional. When trash cans weren't at the curb, sanitation workers would become concerned about the residents. Some would take it upon themselves to wheel the trash can to the sanitation truck if it was visible. I'm sure some sanitation workers are still hospitable. But I believe the number has declined because sanitation hospitality is an added cost. I know people who pay for their can to be taken to the sanitation truck. Some have to pay for excess trash pickup as well.

I also remember life before self-checkouts. Every register was opened. People engaged in conversations while they waited in line. Yes, self-checkouts have made checking out easier for those of us with a handful of items. But do you engage in fruitful conversations and thank the essential worker for their services at self-checkouts?

At self-checkouts there is one cashier monitoring the registers. Sometimes, the cashier is helping others or monitoring the screens to solve check out issues. Occasionally, I might offer greeting words and gestures of gratitude. But, a one-on-one cashier experience is different from a one to ten cashier experience with the cashier being the one.

I admit that I go to self-checkouts to check out quickly. At some stores, self-checkouts are the only way to purchase your items. Why? Let's say, with emphasis: FULL SERVICE CHECKOUTS ARE CLOSED!

As mentioned, I might greet and thank the cashier orally or with a nod. If I'm in a hurry, I get my things and go! In ways, I've succumbed to the fast life of easy checkout. Writing this makes me realize that I need to slow down. I don't like to cook anyway, so it's not like I'm rushing home to prepare a meal. Just thought we need a little humor. Lol.

Now let's do some real time reflection regarding robots replacing humans. Guess what I saw when I went to Sam's Club to shop for our Christmas meal in 2021? As I was walking down the meat department, I saw an autonomous floor-scrubbing robot. The customers stood and stared in awe with me because we didn't see anyone operating it! The automated machine stopped and started when its path was clear. We stared a little longer and continued our shopping in disbelief yet belief. I said to myself, *Another occupation taken and given to a robot.*

All in all, there are pros and cons with the advancement of technology. In future centuries, I wonder how many more computerized occupations will replace humanity. What will be humanity's role in taking care of their dwellings? What is humanity's role in nurturing the world? How will we live out the charge by God to exercise our dominion over the earth, if robots do it for us? Yes, these are some questions to ponder on. Let's write our thoughts here.

_____

_____

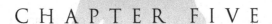

CHAPTER FIVE

VALIDITY TO THE PROPHETIC FUTURE

In August 2021 while I watched *CBS This Morning* with Gayle King, I screamed, and my mouth flew wide open. All I could say was, "Aw… Aw… Aw…." repeatedly between each breath and then I felt myself hold my breath. My next words were, "My Lord and my God. It is true!" Then I screamed *again*. I was home alone, and no one heard me but God and Jesus. My heart pounded. I shed some tears. Took deep breaths and sat on my bed awestricken.

You see on this episode, there was a report on the Telsa Robot. Elon Musk founded Telsa Motors in 2003. He also founded X.com in 1999, which is now PayPal, and SpaceX in 2002. This South African-born American entrepreneur and businessman is creating a humanoid robot. According to *CBS This Morning* and other related resources, the robot is expected to perform boring jobs humanity is expected to do. The anchors had a brief conversation about whether or not the Tesla Robot would wash baby bottles and soothe crying babies. I just cried because that's the role of parents. As a mother, this was my role because I carried my babies in my womb like Mary carried baby Jesus in hers. Our babies were nurtured in the water of our round bellies until birth. Therefore, the thought of a metal humanoid prototype replacing the skin-to-skin cuddles from our newborns is heartbreaking.

The Tesla Bot is expected to go to the grocery store, which validates everything I aforementioned. Some might say that I conjured up all of this after I heard about Elon Musk's humanoid robot; however, that is far from the truth. I started writing this book in 2020. I've had to revise it because we are on the upside of the pandemic with the vaccinations. Because of my procrastination, I was able to see the validity in my prophecy. Some might say it was meant for me to prolong the writing. I would have to disagree because I am supposed to be finished by now. I've made many promises to God month after month to finish, and yet—hmmm—I am still writing. I can't carry this weight past the summer of 2023. I want to be free.

You see freedom is what we experience when we complete the assigned tasks God has told us to do. Freedom is what we experience when the Holy Spirit doesn't have to keep nudging and guiding us to complete our God given assignments. Freedom is what we experience when we are living into our purpose of being the hands and feet of Jesus.

Freedom is what we experience when we believe and have faith in the Trinity—the Father, the Son, and the Holy Spirit. But it's important to know God will continue to call us. The Holy Spirit will continue to nudge us. As faithful disciples of Jesus Christ, we'll never stop being his hands and feet on this earthy Kingdom. Therefore, no matter what tasks or assignments God has for you to complete, it won't be the last. It's only the beginning. Are you ready to get started?

You know, I'm sure people will ridicule and heckle me. But there will be others who will see validity in my prophecy. I'll have some ups and downs about this acceptance. But through it all I know God is with me, and I must be obedient. I'm responsible for my actions. I'm just thankful God speaks to me, and I follow the guidance of the Holy Spirit. Whenever the day comes for me to experience my last day on this earthly kingdom, I want to be assured that I've done what God wanted me to do. I want to hear the words, "Well done my good and faithful servant" (Matthew 25:21a) as I enter through the heavenly gates. Most importantly, I want to see my family and friends again in heaven and angelically watch over my ones that I left on earth. Therefore, doing the will of God is of utmost importance than the experiences I'll encounter after the publication of this journal.

All of this brings to my mind the Apostles' journey after Jesus' ascension. Scripture tells us they stood there looking towards heaven after Jesus ascended. The Apostles didn't know what their next steps would entail, but they knew the importance of being obedient to their rabbi, Jesus.

I've learned from the apostles being obedient doesn't always mean people are going to like what you do or say. I learned from Jesus being obedient can cause a ruckus especially when you're disrupting the norm. All in all, I've learned and experienced people will find fault in those who follow the will of God. But it's okay because their fault finding is irrelevant when our lives are lined up with God's plan. Jesus and the apostles were obedient to the will of God. That is why we are Christians today. Regardless of the pushback they received, they kept walking by faith and not by sight. Because of their perseverance, lives are still being transformed over 2,000 years later. As God is calling me, God is calling you to disrupt the norm too. Change is constant, but accepting change isn't constant. We don't like for our normal routines to be disrupted; therefore, it's challenging to embody the fact that obedience requires sacrifices as we lean more and more into our roles of being followers of Jesus Christ.

When we feel this way, it's important for us to remember Simon Peter and his brother Andrew, as well as brothers, James and John, who left their fishing boats to follow Jesus. These fishermen became fishers of men at Jesus' request. Their lives were interrupted and yet transformed by their rabbi. Life for them was never the same when they left the shore of the Sea of Galilee. Following Jesus means your life will never be the same. As I am writing this book, I know my life will never be the same. But you know what? It's the life God has planned for me. About fifteen years ago, people didn't understand, and I didn't quite understand why God was telling me to leave my home church. As I look back at my journey, God was preparing me to be an ordained elder in the United Methodist Church. I see it clearly now and so do others. Like the disciples, when I made up my mind to follow Jesus, God started accomplishing great things through me. I'm just a vessel used by God to do the will of God. What about you? How is your life aligned with the will of God? Write a one-page reflection.

_____

_____

_____

_____

_____

_____

_____

I love the creation story in the book of Genesis. This story should make us reflect and discern on our obligation to have dominion over the earth. In turn, we should gain a deeper understanding of the will of God not the will of man. It tells us how God created the earth and humanity.

Let's take a look at Genesis 1-2:4.

> *When God began to create the heavens and the earth the earth was without shape or form, it was dark over the deep sea, and God's wind swept over the waters God said, "Let there be light." And so light appeared. God saw how good the light was. God separated the light from the darkness. God named the light Day and the darkness Night. There was evening and there was morning: the first day.*
>
> *God said, "Let there be a dome in the middle of the waters to separate the waters from each other." God made the dome and separated the waters under the dome from the waters above the dome. And it happened in that way. God named the dome Sky. There was evening and there was morning: the second day.*
>
> *God said, "Let the waters under the sky come together into one place so that the dry land can appear." And that's what happened. God named the dry land Earth, and he named the gathered waters Seas. God saw how good it was. God said, "Let the earth grow plant life: plants yielding seeds and fruit trees bearing fruit with seeds inside it, each according to its kind throughout the earth." And that's what happened. The earth produced plant life: plants yielding seeds, each according to its kind, and trees bearing fruit with seeds inside it, each according to its kind. God saw how good it was. There was evening and there was morning: the third day.*
>
> *God said, "Let there be lights in the dome of the sky to separate the day from the night. They will mark events, sacred seasons, days, and years. They will be lights in the dome of the sky to shine on the earth." And that's what happened. God made the stars and two great lights: the larger light to rule over the day and the smaller light to rule over the night. God put them in the dome of the sky to shine on the earth, to rule over the day and over the night, and to separate the light from the darkness. God saw how good it was. There was evening and there was morning: the fourth day.*
>
> *God said, "Let the waters swarm with living things, and let birds fly above the earth up in the dome of the sky." God created the great sea animals and all the tiny living things that swarm in the waters, each according to its kind, and all the winged birds,*

each according to its kind. God saw how good it was. Then God blessed them: "Be fertile and multiply and fill the waters in the seas, and let the birds multiply on the earth." There was evening and there was morning: the fifth day.

God said, "Let the earth produce every kind of living thing: livestock, crawling things, and wildlife." And that's what happened. God made every kind of wildlife, every kind of livestock, and every kind of creature that crawls on the ground. God saw how good it was. Then God said, "Let us make humanity in our image to resemble us so that they may take charge of the fish of the sea, the birds in the sky, the livestock, all the earth, and all the crawling things on earth."

God created humanity in God's own image, in the divine image God created them, male and female God created them. God blessed them and said to them, "Be fertile and multiply; fill the earth and master it. Take charge of the fish of the sea, the birds in the sky, and everything crawling on the ground." Then God said, "I now give to you all the plants on the earth that yield seeds and all the trees whose fruit produces its seeds within it. These will be your food. To all wildlife, to all the birds in the sky, and to everything crawling on the ground to everything that breathe I give all the green grasses for food." And that's what happened. God saw everything he had made: it was supremely good. There was evening and there was morning: the sixth day.

The heavens and the earth and all who live in them were completed. On the sixth day God completed all the work that he had done, and on the seventh day God rested from all the work that he had done. God blessed the seventh day and made it holy, because on it God rested from all the work of creation. This is the account of the heavens and the earth when they were created.

The creation story allows us to see how God can take nothing and make an abundance for humanity because God loves us. Do you believe that we still have an abundance of all in which God created?

Many of the animals God told humanity to take charge over have become extinct because of natural disasters, pollution, and increased ocean travel. Poaching and recreational wildlife hunting are other reasons animals have become extinct. The desire for more power and authority as well as the adrenaline rushes from the *kill* led to an *overkill* of some species. Don't get me wrong: I believe there is nothing wrong with hunting. But if you're going to kill an elephant, then eat the meat, wear the skin, or donate your kill to a needy village or family. If hunters can't eat the meat or use the outer for clothing, why do they commit to the kill? Is it solely for honor, picturesque views, likes, emojis, or to obtain an elite status? Or is the adrenaline rush the drive and thrive?

I'm sure God would love for humanity to think twice—ask God for advice—before shooting a device to kill animals. Doing this will assist you in not losing sight of what is right.

WOW! It took me a few minutes to think of that rhyme because I wanted to incorporate some validity in the rhyming words. What do you think about the rhyme regarding validity? Did it make you reflect on more than animals?

You know we have opportunities to make just decisions. In 1 Kings chapter 3, there is a story about King David's son, Solomon. God granted his request for wisdom because he didn't ask for longevity, wealth, or power to defeat his enemies. Solomon wanted to be an exceptional king like his father. Both made mistakes; however, God used them to glorify God's name. Knowing this should help us to understand that wise people make mistakes. Yet, wisdom recognizes the prompting of the Holy Spirit to repent of your sins. Are you praying for wisdom to build up the kingdom of God so that you can effectively honor the two greatest commandments: the love of God and the love of neighbor?

In January 2022, a portion of my sermon entailed what it means to love God with all our heart, soul, and mind and to love our neighbors as ourselves. This is what I preached:

> *We hear these two commandments over and over but what do they mean?*
>
> *Loving God with all your **heart means** to love God with our emotions. In doing so, we love God in good times and through the bad times. We love God when we wait patiently and anxiously for answers to our prayers. And whatever the answer is to our prayers, we still love God. We may not agree with the answers, but we know God knows what's best for us.*

*When we think about love we usually stop with our heart. But when we love God, we must love with our soul as well. Loving God with our **soul means** we love God when we don't feel like it. Our soul takes us farther than our heart in loving God. It moves us to having a grace filled relationship with God.*

*Loving God with our **mind means** more than just thinking about God. It encompasses us thinking more like Jesus and thinking less of our own sinful thoughts as well as acting upon them. Jesus wants us to know nothing should be held back when we love God!!... To love our neighbor as ourselves means we decide to love humanity like we love ourselves.*

The sermon series was undergirded by the book *A Disciple's Path* by Justin Larosa and James Harnish. Collierville United Methodist Church in Collierville, Tennessee began its all-church study in January 2022, and this is the study we chose to remind us of our membership vows. Letting you know the date of the study makes you aware of the fact I am still writing. I'm working you all…. I'm working…

You know—the pandemic gave us an opportunity to renew our covenant with God by reflecting on the two greatest commandments. When we were sent back home, we had a chance to reevaluate ourselves and turn back to God. Some of us took a strong stance, and said, "I never left God." However, God gave me the following prophetic message while I am writing:

You did when you didn't acknowledge my presence and gifts of grace to you. When you were blessed, did you bless others with your abundance? or in the extra?

When you were angry, did you talk to me? Or apologize to your neighbor?"

When you were ill, did you acknowledge the gift of life before the illness? Or did you just pray for healing?

God gave me the message you just read as I was writing. I think it's necessary for me to leave you some lines to answer God.

_____

_____

REVEREND TONDALA L. HAYWARD

After God gave me the message, I did some reflection myself. I couldn't say yes wholeheartedly to all these God asked questions. What about you?

Unfortunately, many times we must experience a live-changing moment for us to renew our covenant with God. Recently, the life-changing moment for the world was the Coronavirus. During Safer at Home, we prayed fervently to Jesus to ask God to save us. We prayed for first responders, people who were ill around the world, and those who weren't. We prayed for the pandemic to be over. We prayed for the death rate to decline as it was continuing to rise steadily.

We prayed fervently and God answered our prayers! Over four years later, the Coronavirus, aka COVID-19, is still present in the world. However, the death toll isn't as high, but the Omicron and other variants are still seeping into the world. I don't believe God sent this virus to the world like the plagues that were sent in Egypt. But God did tell me the following after stopping and reflecting just now.

This is what God said, *I did send an angel to stop the virus, but no one listened. The truth will come out.*

I stopped, gasped, shook my head, thought about the lives lost. Shook my head again and began to feel overwhelmingly sad. Then, I said aloud to God, "Well, God, we *shall know the truth and the truth shall set us free*" (John 8:32). The truth in how the virus originated will be fully known to us one day in this life or the next. However, we do know this truth: the virus is still dwelling among us today.

COVID has taken the life of family and friends. Some of you who are reading this book have been infected, know someone who has been infected, and/or lost family and friends due to COVID. I hope believing in the resurrection gives you some peace and comfort. Especially if you couldn't attend a traditional celebration of life service for the deceased.

I believe we should take a moment and pray for those who've lost their lives due to COVID, those who are ill, first responders, and other. Let's make our petitions to God. Please feel free to list the name of anyone who was infected or died because of the Coronavirus.

For your loved ones who transitioned to the Heavenly Kingdom, may this Scripture give you comfort and peace:

> *Then I saw a new heaven and a new earth, for the former heaven and the former earth had passed away, and the sea was no more. I saw the holy city, New Jerusalem, coming down out of heaven from God, made ready as a bride beautifully dressed for her husband. I heard a loud voice from the throne say, "Look! God's dwelling is here with humankind. He will dwell with them, and they will be his peoples. God himself will be with them as their God. He will wipe away every tear from their eyes. Death will be no more. There will be no mourning, crying, or pain anymore, for the former things have passed away." Then the one seated on the throne said, "Look! I'm making all things new." He also said, "Write this down, for these words are trustworthy and true." Then he said to me, "All is done. I am the Alpha and the Omega, the beginning and the end. To the thirsty I will freely give water from the life-giving spring. Those who emerge victorious will inherit these things. I will be their God, and they will be my sons and daughters.*
>
> Revelation 21:1-7

CHAPTER SIX

NO ONE KNOWS THE DAY OR THE HOUR

Let us look at Matthew 24:36-44:

> *But nobody knows when that day or hour will come, not the heavenly angels and not the Son. Only the Father knows. As it was in the time of Noah, so it will be at the coming of the Human One. In those days before the flood, people were eating and drinking, marrying, and giving in marriage, until the day Noah entered the ark. They didn't know what was happening until the flood came and swept them all away. The coming of the Human One will be like that. At that time there will be two men in the field. One will be taken and the other left. Two women will be grinding at the mill. One will be taken and the other left. Therefore, stay alert! You don't know what day the Lord is coming. But you understand that if the head of the house knew at what time the thief would come, he would keep alert and wouldn't allow the thief to break into his house. Therefore, you also should be prepared, because the Human One will come at a time you don't know.*

After reading this I asked God, "Why should I write about the Second Coming of the Messiah when I am included in the no one knows?

This is what God said, to me: *I have chosen you to tell the story of what it will look like when my Son will come back again. You don't know the day or the hour, but you do know the earth won't move or shatter. People will be in an uproar. There will be wars and rumor of more wars. A remnant of people will have enough power to try to destroy the world where Christianity has taken over. Yes, there will be more Christians in the world than there are now. These people will be like the High Priest and Pharisees, who rejected my Son. They will call themselves the Reluctants because they will doubt my Son. But grace and mercy will keep some of them from being casted and burned in hell. Some will be saved, and others will become like Paul and King David. But there is only going to be one Mary, the mother of Jesus and one earthly father, Joseph, who died of old age. There will only be one beloved Son.*

After sitting and reflecting on these words from God, I'm just astonished. I've read them over and over again to get some understanding. This is what I've derived from my reflections. I asked God to determine if I'm correct and God said, *Correct.*

As I continued to meditate and discern all that God gave me, I asked God why will people be in an uproar with wars? God said, *People will be in an uproar because the world will be more unified in color but not spirit.*

While God was telling me this, I saw a vision of more people of color than whites. Then I asked God what does this mean? How can this happen?

God replied, *Because of natural disasters, interracial marriages which come from the desire to seek the outcast. Don't you know I created you with a free will to test my strengths and power?*

Then I said, "But we were told not to put you to a test." God said *test me for the righteous in me and the righteousness in yourself.* I asked, "What does that mean?"

God said, *You were created in my image; therefore, you are righteous. When you leave me righteousness is in you because I'm righteous and will never leave you. We dwell in each other even though you may forsake me at times. The test is for purity. How pure is soul? Will you resist doing good even though others are doing wrong? Will you deny me even though I have never denied you? Even though you deny me with your mind you will never deny me with your heart. When the heart aligns with the mind then you are righteous like me. Until then you are righteousness."*

When God finished speaking to me, I Googled *righteous* and *righteousness* for more clarity. Here are my results from dictionary.com:

Righteous means acting in an upright, moral way; virtuous.
Righteousness means the quality or state of being righteous.

From my Google and what God told me, here are the simple explanations. The root word for righteous and righteousness is *right*, which is in accordance with what is good, proper, truth, or just. Thus, God is right and therefore righteous. Since humanity is made in the image of God, we have qualities of being righteous. As a result, we identify with righteousness because we have a state of being righteous. Humanity isn't righteous because we have a free will to choose whether or not we want to engage in right or wrong behavior.

Did this explanation give you some clarity? If not, call a friend or two for further discussion. Also, talk to God, reflect and wait patiently for God to answer. Then reflect on all of what God said to you.

When I finished my righteous and righteousness Googling, I continued my conversation with God. I asked God about the people of color because I know God told me about robots in the future. When I did, I saw a vision of how robots will be used as household assistants. Then God said, *This is not my way I chose for you. You are to have dominion over the world by being hands and feet. Your hands and feet. Maybe I created you too wise that you have used your wisdom to go against my provisions for you.*

I thought, *We are trying to be wiser than the Creator. Again, how can the created be wiser than the Creator? Who have we become? I know we try to outwit each other.* But we can't outwit God, our Creator.

I asked God again about the people of color and robots. God gave me this vision with words, *As robots are created for military warfare. They will begin to do policing as the need for patrol officers declines. These robots will be programed to target people of color who will be the majority population. The stereotypes programmed in the robot's software will make them bias. People will protest, but the Reluctants will be the robots' allies.*

I thought, *People will be partnering with humanoid robots to go against the will of God. They will want to protect and elevate their radical behavior. I guess the Reluctants will love their humanlike robots as their neighbors instead of humans.*

I just sat in awe with tears rolling down my cheeks and just felt very strange. Words can't totally describe my sitting in the presence of God feeling. I felt warm, open, submissive, and shocked. I can't describe the rest.

As I continued to sit in the presence of God - God started speaking to me again: *War will begin. The earth I created will begin to become desolate. People will die, including children. Their brain parts will be used for research. People will begin to study humanity because their works will be no more as I wished them to be. Their labor will be vanished, and others are trying to figure out what did humanity do from things of the old. Therefore, archive your works so people will know your deeds even though it may be lost but make an effort on my behalf.*

After reflecting on all that God has revealed to me, I wondered, *Will there be farmers, bus drivers, railroads, and conductors, writing utensils, gasoline, paper, books, coins, paper currency, keys…. Will people go to the doctor to receive care? Telehealth is becoming all too real. Will robots perform all surgeries? If this is what the future holds, the need for surgical teams will be limited or obsolete.*

My mind just began to wonder and ask questions. What are your thoughts?

I believe, we are going to destroy ourselves by wanting to make things easier and assessable for day-to-day living. The first thought which came to me is the remote. During my childhood years, I was the remote control. Were you one too? _____ In other words, I changed the television. But now, we let the remote do the work for us. If it's lost, we usually become frustrated and won't watch TV. We'll cut it off before we push buttons on the TV to change the channels. Actually, most satellite and cable television services won't work if we don't use their remote.

After thinking of the many times, I didn't pass the "No Remote Lazy Challenge," which is to change your TV without the remote, I began to reflect again. God told me: *Because the earth is left desolate, humanity as I created has been destroyed, my Son will come to begin my Second Coming.*

I asked God what they will see and how the earth will look.

God said, *My Son will tell them how to take care of the soil. I will need to create new creatures for the sea.*

When God told me about creating new sea creatures, I became saddened and leaned back in my chair with disbelief and a broken heart. Then, I saw the seas appearing in my vision looking black and tarry. My eyes filled with tears as I imagined dolphins, whales, sharks, sea fish, and other sea creatures vanishing. But God said, *Don't cry. These are my creations that I formed, and I will fix it like I always do. You will help me from heaven. You will be one of my great prophets and will see the day all of this will happen. You will come down from the heavens and be with those who I chose to make all again the way it should be. You are my Elijah, my Moses, and you will be with those who are less fortunate. Your spirit will lead them to victory and peace to be saved.*

When God told me this, I saw myself leading children and teens who were hiding in a cave to safety. They were hiding from robots, war, and the further destruction of earth. The children were dingy and frightened. Yet, they were waiting and had a deep desire to be saved. The children didn't know how they were going to be saved, *but God knew.*

God sent me to save them so that I can see the validity in my prophecy. As I was writing, God told me, *You have always had a heart to help those in need.*

I thought to myself there is a vast array of work to do on God's earthy kingdom, and I want to engage in it. While patiently thinking and envisioning endless possibilities on how to be a servant leader who work alongside other disciples, my heart smiled. Then I was reminded that my appointment limits the words I can say, and the servant opportunities that I can engage in. Not to my surprise, but our sovereign God heard my silently spoken words and said, *I'll remove you so you can do more of my will.*

You know, God always keeps a promise. Since I am still writing and talking to God to make sure I'm accurate in this prophetic journal, in January 2023, I was appointed to campus ministry. I am connecting with people from different ethnic groups, socioeconomic status, and gender. I am very grateful to be a campus minister. The college students are growing spiritually and learning life skills to help with adulting. Serving those who live on the margins of society and being social justice advocates are discipleship tasks of many young adults. For these reasons and more, I am grateful to work alongside the college students. People are hurting in this world. The time is now to advocate for the oppressed. Charity is good but disrupting the systems that causes people to be poor is also being the hands and feet of Jesus. As follower of Jesus, we must be obedient to God not humanity.

Now, let's get back to the children, who are waiting and wanting to be saved.

I saw in a vision: the children were dingy and frightened. Yet, they were waiting and wanting to be saved. They didn't know how or when they were going to be saved, *but God knew.* When I came into their presence, I held out my hand and a girl grabbed it. The others followed us as I walked them through something which looked like a cave. As we continued to walk through the cave, the darkness became denser and denser and denser. Then all of a sudden, we walked out of a cave into bright light and land that was habitable. All of us smiled and looked around with physical and spiritual glee. When I think of this new land, I can't help but think of Moses and the Israelites. God will prepare and save a piece of the earth for the children. They will dwell on land flowing with milk and honey. In that moment, I felt my trust in God as I was leading the children to a safe, nurturing, and prosperous home. You see, even in heaven the angels are expected to obey God. The angelic beings don't have the full details of their mission. For this reason, I didn't know where I was going, but I kept leading the children with God's help. I guess, life in heaven has some similarities like earth regarding obedience to our Heavenly Father.

Then God spoke again: *The earth will begin anew. Roots will be planted and toiled. My people will remember me and come back to me, and a new earth will begin again. My Son will bring them back to me. He won't die again, but he will ascend after my toil is done. There will be a new Jerusalem, neither slave nor free. All will belong to me. Another coming will take place. But you won't lead them but will be mentioned. Someone will rise like you for the Third Coming and the third book of revelation.*

I thought will there be a second and third Bible with new stories about the Second and Third Coming, and God said: *Yes, and there is only One Son with many works. He will always save my people because he is the Savior. Apart from him, I am nothing to the earth since he brings life to the earth. He walks where no man can walk or speak languages where no one can fathom. He loves like no other. Be still and know I'm God and will keep you in my heart forever and ever.*

All I can think of now is, Oh, Lord, how excellent is your name in all the earth. Your Son suffered and died to save us from our sins. You resurrected him so that we can have a new life on earth by way of repentance because of your unconditional love for us. You give humanity numerous times to correct our wrongdoing even though we are greedy, envious, and have desires to make things perfect and easier. The continuous mandate for humanoid robots to replace humanity will lead us to destruction. People will protest their production but won't win.

My heart laments the day when the earth will begin to be destroyed. It will be very slow and unnoticeable to the human eye because it will inch into becoming a way of life. I pray for those who will hide to keep their sanity and their humanity. They will be the treasured ones who knows how the earth used to be toiled. They will know about Jesus and will assist Jesus in the Second Coming. They will be young because the old will die from the fumes. Technology will be no more but will rise again and default millions of years after the Second Coming. We will recycle our ways.

The Third Coming will do more with outer space, God said to me. After hearing this, I sat with widened eyes in awe while continuing to type these words from God: *"Why leave earth and I have created all the planets and those outer beings? Protect what I have given you and there will be no need for a Third Coming but you won't listen to me. A new baby will be born for the Third Coming. You will see the birth and will be at hand. All these things treasure in your heart my beloved daughter who I called by name to bring the Good News of cheer and sorrow to the world."*

God blew my mind with the Second Coming! Now, for God to tell me about the Third Coming and it would come into fruition with space left me flabbergasted. I guess humanity will become more inquisitive about outer space. Yes, we will learn from how humanoid robots replaced the daily living of humanity, but free will and intelligence will lead to the Third Coming. God didn't give me any more details. I don't know the day or hour for the Second and Third Comings. However, I do know we need to prepare ourselves in this lifetime by resisting the extensive expansion of artificial intelligence in relation to humanoid robots, if humanity doesn't want to get to the point of being near extinction.

The possibility of us becoming extinct makes me flow a wail of tears. The first thing I reflect on is prehistoric life. My mind eases back in time to when I studied humans being hunters and gathers. Images of dinosaurs and other prehistoric animals came to my mind. Thinking about prehistoric life makes me realize there is truth in this prophecy. During my tearing, I ask the question again: "Why me?"

My response from God was, *It's your heart.* I cried some more and began to dry my eyes. My next thought was that angels don't get old. I began reflecting on Revelation 21. Here it is again:

> *Then I saw a new heaven and a new earth, for the former heaven and the former earth had passed away, and the sea was no more. I saw the holy city, New Jerusalem, coming down out of heaven from God, made ready as a bride beautifully dressed for her husband. I heard a loud voice from the throne say, "Look! God's dwelling is here with humankind. He will dwell with them, and they will be his peoples. God himself will be with them as their God. He will wipe away every tear from their eyes. Death will be no more. There will be no mourning, crying, or pain anymore, for the former things have passed away." Then the one seated on the throne said, "Look! I'm making all things new." He also said, "Write this down, for these words are trustworthy and true." Then he said to me, "All is done. I am the Alpha and the Omega, the beginning, and the end. To the thirsty I will freely give water from*

the life-giving spring. Those who emerge victorious will inherit these things. I will be their God, and they will be my sons and daughters. But for the cowardly, the faithless, the vile, the murderers, those who commit sexual immorality, those who use drugs and cast spells, the idolaters, and all liars—their share will be in the lake that burns with fire and sulfur. This is the second death."

I began to wonder about the Second Coming being like heaven on earth, since it will look different in future centuries. I mentioned the sea will become black and tarry. The children will be saved; therefore, their tears will be wiped away because they won't fear death from the war. The children are God's Sons and Daughters who will be saved by the Alpha and Omega.

Again, heaven will come on earth because the former earth has passed away and the sea was no more. I know that I've given you a lot to reflect on. It's time to journal. My heart becomes broken every time I think about the events that will lead to the Second Coming. That is why, I know you may be broken from shock, disgust, belief, or unbelief and more.

Write your thoughts here and rest. You can continue to read this devotional tomorrow or the next day.

_____

_____

CHAPTER SEVEN

WHERE DO WE GO FROM HERE?

First, I'm not God, and I don't know the day or hour Jesus will come for the Second Coming. To know means, I have all the attributes of God and I don't. As I'm writing this, I thought, *Jesus doesn't have all the attributes of God. After all, did he resurrect himself or did God?*

To this clearer, I am fully human. Jesus was fully human and fully divine. God is all divine and works in the supernatural, which is a realm in which we have no authority to function because we don't have the power and ability in the flesh to function in the supernatural.

The supernatural is a realm in which Jesus functions due to his genetic makeup. Because of his human qualities, he couldn't resurrect himself. He didn't use his divine power to free himself from the cross. Instead, he succumbed to the agony of being crucified like the two thieves who hung with him. However, Jesus was innocent and committed no crime. Power coupled with jealousy will make you blind to the truth like it did the religious leaders.

In reality, the truth hurts at times. Instead of accepting the truth, some people resist it and accept lies because it makes them feel better. However, the truth stands firm and bold with the presence of God. The truth will overcome Satan's lies at all times. Jesus overcame death with the resurrection. His followers truly believed he was the Son of God when they saw him at his post resurrection appearances.

But you shall know the truth and the truth shall set you free. —John 8:32

When Jesus resurrected the widow's son and Lazarus, he was working in his divine realm. Healing the woman with the issue of blood, lepers, giving sight to the blind, and other miraculous healings were all done in the divine authority of the supernatural realm in which his Heavenly Father exists. I pondered on the genes of Jesus' genetic makeup in regard to him being divine. Remember, Mary was impregnated by the Holy Spirit. There are no genes to connect Jesus to his fully divine character. Mary's egg that was impregnated gives Jesus the human character.

So, I asked God, "How did Jesus become fully human, since Mary and Joseph didn't consummate their marriage?" As I sat and meditated, I was led back to the Garden of Eden. God formed Adam from the dust of the earth and placed him in the Garden of Eden. After God realized Adam shouldn't be alone in the Garden of Eden, he formed a suitable helper for him from his rib. When Adam woke up from his deep sleep, he was awakened to a surprise. There was Eve standing in his midst to help him toil the land and be his helpmate.

God took dust to form Adam and breathe into his nostrils the breath of life. Then God took a rib from Adam to form Eve. I pondered and came to the belief that surely the Holy Spirit can fertilize Mary's eggs, which moved through the waters to rest in her uterus. I concluded that Jesus was nurtured in the womb of his mother, cared for by his earthly father, Joseph, and formed by his Heavenly Father through the power of the Holy Spirit. Jesus is fully human from the uterus of Mary and fully divine by being impregnated from the Holy Spirit.

As I'm writing this, God said, *He is mine. I created him so that you can have a glimpse of me.*

I asked God why having a glimpse of him was important.

God replied, *The Holy Bible.*

I was waiting on more but that was all I was told.

But with analytical perceptions, we can imagine who God is in the Old Testament. Creation shows God as being all powerful, loving, graceful, and much more - all in all - God is *Omniscient*. Since God knows everything, God knew Eve ate from the tree of good and evil, and Adam and

Eve's son, Cain, killed Abel. We know God as *All Knowing* and *Sovereign*. God heard the prayers of the Israelites and answered them even though they weren't always obedient. They denied God, but when they became captive in Egypt and Babylon, they cried out to God for help and God heard their cries. God's unconditional love is always available to humanity. God's grace is always covering us even when we don't know it or deserve it. David, Solomon, and Jonah's stories and many others speak to the grace, mercy, and forgiving heart of God. Therefore, in the Old Testament, we know who God is by God's miracles and compassionate character.

How do you see God in the Old Testament?

_____

In the New Testament, we know who God is by the life and works of Jesus. Since God came to the earth incarnate in Jesus Christ, we see God fully in human form. Jesus's fully divine form allows us to visualize the supernatural character of God.

How do you see God in the New Testament?

_____

Again, where do we go from here? I've asked God this question many times. When I reflect on this question. I think about a book I started writing with the same title, *Where Do We Go From Here?* I began to write the book because of the bullying I was seeing at school among the students. I was trying to find a way to help students with their pain. Many times, people bully others because of their own pain. The saying is true: Hurt people hurt people. Usually, they hurt people who they are close to which are usually family and friends. Of course, I didn't finish it because fear of it wouldn't sell and not thinking I was good enough to be a published author. I also became busy doing other God-centered things. Earlier, I alluded to the fact that avoidance is real because of fear. In other words, I focused on another task instead of what God was calling me to do at that moment. Fear and feeling like I'm not worthy enough to be a writer has been my pitfall.

I'm constantly thinking and asking myself the same question: *Who would read it?* I'm thinking the same thing right now: *Who is going to read this book*, The Second Coming? Well, if you made it to this page, I would say *you*!! What do you think about this book thus far?

_____

I am extremely grateful you're reading and journaling. I have given you a lot to ponder, but it isn't my doing. *It is all of God's doing!* I'm just a vessel used to carry out the will of God.

Let's get back to where we go from here.

One thought I have is that we should wholeheartedly live into the two greatest commandments: "You must love the Lord your God with all your heart, with all your being, and with all your mind. This is the first and greatest commandment. And the second is like it: You must love your neighbor as you love yourself..." (Matthew 22:37-39).

As I am reflecting on the two greatest commandments, I began to wonder how can we express our love to God in response to all that I have written. While sitting at my desk in a relaxing posture, I can't help but think about God's creation of the earth and humanity. Loving God means we will want to be exceptional stewards of all that God has given us. Therefore, we are excellent land- and water-keepers, which means we should be cognizant of how we're destroying God's creations. In doing so, we have to become aware of how humanity is going to be nearly extinct.

I guess you're wondering how humanity is going to be less of the population. Well, let me tell you! You see it's going to become all too real of how humanoid robots will slowly progress to taking over the life of humanity. At first, it's going to be gleeful and satisfying to know you don't have to do yard work, housekeeping, pay for automotive service, cook, fight in combat, checkout your groceries, walk your dog, pay for a trainer .... and.... The list can go on and on and on....

But, what happens when there isn't a yard to mow or till because grass, flowers, bushes, and trees will be no more?

_____

What happens when there are no children in the homes or mates for procreation because expenditures are replaced with robotic maintenance?

_____

I believe humanity will love the extra time given back to them because their daily tasks will be less. Robot maids, who are more intelligent than Rosie from the Jetsons, will complete household chores, shopping, and parenting. However, what happens to households who can't

THE SECOND COMING OF THE MESSIAH

afford a robot maid? Is this going to become a new bias, which will lead to additional stereotypes and discrimination?

Now let's ponder on robots replacing tasks in which nurturing parents are created to do. I guarantee you that someone is going to create a robot to feed an infant the nursed milk from the mother, change a soiled diaper, and speak in the voice tone of the mother to provide soothing touches so that the baby will be comforted. Add the voice of the father to express fatherly love will make the presumed parental role complete. Developers will say the male voice can replace absentee fathers or vice versa with a female voice replacing absentee mothers. When humanity live into these moments, they may think Human Replacement Theory is acceptable because we're wanting more time to do other things. We often complain there isn't enough time in the day to complete our daily household tasks, work, and have leisure time. As a result, human replacement will be the answer.

I know that I am right with the Human Replacement theory. Since I've procrastinated on writing, this book passed my self-determined deadline. On January 5, 2022 another segment aired on *CBS This Morning* about artificial intelligence which included humanoid robots. The robot is being designed by Engineer Arts. I would like to say they look so humanlike that it's breathtaking and yet scary. On the show, I saw a robot massager from *Massage Robotics* removing the kinks and soreness out of a lady's back. To be honest, the last time I got a massage from Gould's, I enjoyed my conversation with the masseuse. On *CBS This Morning*, I didn't see any type of conversations between the humanoid robot and the client. I'm sure they can program the robot to communicate. But will it be a genuine conversation? Will a robot speak to us with emotions? Additionally on this episode, co-host Nate Burleson said, "When it comes to robots, I think I've seen this in a movie before, and it didn't turn out good." [1]

Well, I believe it will work out good for a while until humanity gets greedy and lazy and demand more and more from robots and less from humanity. A demand in supply of robots may lead to the birthing of less humans. What are your thoughts about the Human Replacement Theory?

God is telling me there is going to be a direct correlation to the replacement of humanoid robots with humanity. Everything prophesied in Matthew 24 will come into fruition. I would like to

---

[1] https://www.youtube.com/watch?v=lEZLYwFnkMc

ask you to read Matthew 24 with a commentary at hand to help you with understanding. My favorite New Testament commentaries are *Life Application Bible Commentary.* I have all these little green books in my home office. I use them quite often in sermon preparation. You may have a favorite. But if you don't, go to Amazon and purchase a *Life Application Bible Commentary* on the Gospel of Matthew. You definitely won't regret it! Who knows? You might spark an interest in purchasing more commentaries to gain a better understanding of God's Holy Word, the Bible.

As I mentioned, read Matthew 24 with a commentary, and reflect on it for a day or two. Then answer these questions.

What are you thinking?

_____

Who is the Human One?

_____

Where is humanity?

_____

When will the Human one come?

_____

Finally, how can we prolong the destruction of the human world so that it takes longer to become more of an artificial intelligence robotic world?

_____

Any other questions and thoughts?

_____

_____

CHAPTER EIGHT

MY THOUGHTS & REFLECTIONS

While continuing to reflect on all God has told me, I keep going back to the Safer at Home policy during the peak of the Coronavirus-COVID 19. Quarantine allowed us to spend a magnitude of time with our families. We prayed and stayed closely knit together. I'm actually waiting on data to see if there is going to be a baby boom. Couples spent a lot of time together rekindling what was lost, reimagining how to spend their time with each other, and appreciating each other's companionship in many ways.

But I must also be realistic in mentioning domestic violence increased. Some of the reasons were spouses and significant others weren't able to release their stressors by working at their job, meeting friends at sport bars, in-person peer interactive conversations, exercising at their favorite gym, or engage in other stress relievers. Employment uncertainty was definitely a stressor. To be honest, some people didn't feel safer at home because of verbal and physical abuse. If this is you today, *you* don't deserve to be treated this way. It is okay to seek help by finding a shelter and/ or calling the police. I'm sure you've been praying. Now, it's time to take an enormous leap of faith. Fear can keep you captive. It took hold of me in writing this book. I worked through my fears and procrastination. That is why, I am feeling a sense of liberation. You can feel it too when you take the necessary steps to freedom. Yes, our fears are different; but it's fear. To overcome fear, you need to always believe: God is with you and will provide a way out of every situation. You don't want the way out to be death on earth and life in the heavenly kingdom. However, you do want it to be death to physical and verbal abuse on earth and a liberated life on earth.

Go get your life back!

As many may have felt safe at home and while others have not, the word *security* comes to mind. We have mental securities because we depend on our loved ones to provide for our needs. We have home security systems to prevent break-ins. We have spiritual securities in believing God will take care of all our needs. Psalm 55:22 tell us, "Cast your burden on the Lord—he will support you! God will never let the righteous be shaken!"

Usually with every home security system, a reset button is accessible to the customers. These start-over buttons are pressed for troubleshooting purposes. Because of Jesus' death on the cross, we can reset our lives by way of repentance. After we repent of our sins, we reset our lives to continue our journey towards Christian perfection. However, we understand we'll never be perfect. Resetting gives us opportunities to get things right by striving to live a better life with Jesus as our role model. The Holy Spirit as our guide and God as our parent. In other words, our Heavenly Father.

Knowing what you know now about the Human Replacement Theory, the questions are:

How can humanity reset their priorities? How can the future of human existence become our priority? What is your role as a follower of Jesus?

_____

_____

Yes, it's inevitable that the advancement in technology will replace humanity's occupations. But should humanoid robots solely replace the duties and responsibilities of parents, guardians, teachers, police, postal workers, drivers, custodians, pilots, medical professionals, gardeners, soldiers, parking attendants, and......and....and................?

_____

_____

When this happens—not *if* this happens—humanity will be broken. As the Human Replacement Theory comes into fruition, the world will gradually decline as humans lose their power and authority.

Because of God's unconditional love for humanity, God will be waiting to send Jesus to mend the broken pieces. When the Savior comes a second time, there will be a new Jerusalem. A light who will shine in the darkness. Wars will cease. Justice will reign for the unjust. Stories will be told about the existence of humanity. These stories will include moments in which humanity took pride in their worth. There will be new parables to teach lessons so that humanity won't be destroyed again on earth. These stories will include the prophets, who will be people we have studied in history. Stories will also be told about people who promoted genocide, homicide, insurrections, and murder to gain power and authority. These people were led by Satan.

Jesus will tell the stories of the good which came out of every turmoil. The stories will give humanity hope like the Bible does today. It will also give humanity warnings and tell of consequences about what will happen when humanity is disobedient. God will have to create the earth again because of its destruction. God's Son, Jesus, will come to do the work. Humanity will be birthed again. This time with natural births not from dust. There will be a new creation of people who will follow Jesus. Oral tradition, scribes, and another Bible will be birthed because Jesus' second coming will need to be told for future generations to believe in Christianity. The Bible will speak on how fire and destruction consumed the earth. However, Jesus will consume the fire and bring humanity—God's Genesis creations—back to life. No chaos, war, desolation, nation, kingdom, or natural disaster will be able to stand up against our Lord and Savior.

The Second Coming is real, and we have an opportunity to prolong it, *but* not postpone it. The Human Replacement Theory is going to happen; however, we don't know the date. To know means we are like God, and we're not. No one knows the day or hour when Jesus will come. Again, I don't know the date. But, I know about humanity's involvement in it and what the world will look like when Jesus appears for his second coming. Each generation will do their part to make this prophecy become a reality.

It's time to journal your thoughts, emotions, questions...

_____

CHAPTER NINE

WORRIED ABOUT THE WRONG REPLACEMENT THEORY

On May 14, 2022, Payton Gendon killed ten people and wounded three others at TOPS friendly Supermarket in Buffalo, New York. The investigation of this brutal federal hate crime revealed Payton's actions were motivated by his belief that Black people are replacing white people.

If you've been reading my book thoroughly with me, you'll see there will be more people of color in the future. However, it's not due to the fact of immigrants migrating to the United States. Nor is the increase population of people of color due to the fact of there being more people of color in leadership. I've heard through grapevine conversations that these two reasons are leading to the increase of the Brown and Black populations.

You know I believe one word is leading to the change in ethnic population percentages.

The one word is LOVE!!

I have often asked myself why do I see more interracial couples? I believe racial barriers have been broken. Ethnicities have realized that *love conquers all* barriers, biases, stereotypes, and history. When slave ships were brought over to the Americas, Africans were called heathens. Yet, white men fell in love with the skin tone and physique of the women. Now let's be honest, all masters and overseers were not passionately in love with African women because many were raped;

however, they loved being curious. And this curiosity increased the master's slave population on his plantation. Most of the biracial children born from this sexual experience worked in the house and many received privileges, since the master's blood pumped through their veins and organs. On the other hand, some masters, men and women, fell in love with their slaves, while others just sought a different ride.

However, throughout the years, the strongholds that kept the intertwining of ethnicities from sharing their love for each other is slowly dissipating, and it will continue. Again, *love conquers all* barriers, biases, stereotypes, and history.

1 Corinthians 13:4-8 tells us, *"Love is patient, love is kind, it isn't jealous, it doesn't brag, it isn't arrogant, it isn't rude, it doesn't seek its own advantage, it isn't irritable, it doesn't keep a record of complaints, it isn't happy with injustice, but it is happy with the truth. Love puts up with all things, trusts in all things, hopes for all things, endures all things. Love never fails."*

Could it truly be people have realized the heart overcomes racial barriers when determining who you want to be in relationship with? You know - People really want to give and receive love no matter the ethnicity, gender, age, economic status, disability, medical history etc. What are your thoughts?

Thus, it's not the Critical Race Theory that people should be worried about. It is Human Replacement Theory. Let's have some real talk for a moment....

To take the Critical Race Theory from curriculums mean much of Black history will be taken away. It's already minimally taught in schools. I was hoping the Black Lives Matter historical social justice movement during the Covid pandemic would be in the new history books. However, I don't think it will because people believe Black Lives Matter undergirds the Critical Race Theory.

As an African American female, who is clergy, mother, social justice advocate, sister, friend, aunt, grandmother, cousin, leader, and so much more ...

BLACK LIVES MATTER IS RELEVANT AND IT GIVES ME RELEVANCE!!

Because of the inhumane treatment of Black people for centuries, this social justice movement was birthed. For those who are having trouble understanding the purpose of this global justice liberating nonprofit, you need to ask yourself, *Why do people need to say Black Lives Matter in the twenty-first century? I've heard we elected Barack Obama as president and Kamala Harris as vice president. We also have elected Black male and female city, county, and state representatives.*

All of this is true. However, stories need to be told about the transatlantic slave trade and the discriminative disparities in education, housing, employment, incarceration, and healthcare systems in relation to people of color.

In my opinion if these stories aren't kept in the forefront, Black and Brown people will begin to believe their experiences with discrimination, bias, racism, and stereotypes are a way of life. As a result, history journeys backward to Jim Crow instead of forward to a beloved community.

Personally, I need to know my history because Black History encourages, empowers, and motivates me to continue the fight for equity. My history allows me to see the mistreatment of my ancestors because of their skin color. Their stories give me hope, perseverance, self-worth, black pride, faith, assurance, and confidence. I respect the Civil Rights Movement, and everyone who had a role in the passing of The Civil Rights Act of 1964. On the contrary, I understand the necessity of telling white people about the pain associated with racism. After they listen, many apologize, have a desire to be in collaboration, lead the collaboration and/or they want to be involved in transformative action steps to dismantle racism.

I am still trying to understand how the same people who say they love me, don't believe in the Black Lives Matter Movement nor care to say the words, "Black Lives Matter." And yet, I love them with agape love. Acknowledging and knowing this, always brings tears to my eyes since I wonder – Do you really love all who God created me to be? which includes the color of my skin, my advocacy, my character, preaching, teaching, friendship, leadership, and prophetic voice.

As an elementary teacher and pastor, I learned how to truly accept people as they are. Why is it difficult for some people to accept me as I am? Consequently, why is it difficult for people to accept God made us different to showcase the many expressions of Jesus Christ.

As I previously mentioned, there will be more Black and Brown people in the world; therefore, you might expect racism will become obsolete.

Yes, I did say the aforementioned. However, history will repeat itself, if we don't learn from it and want to change it for the betterment of the world. Therefore, I can't help but wonder what oppression and power would look like in the next centuries. Will Black and Brown people become the oppressors to continue to perpetuate systemic racism? After all, light skinned and dark-skinned slaves had different roles on plantations which created tension and discrimination within their own race. Black people were pitted against each other. This disgruntlement is still present.

In society today, the world has seen the video of Tyre Nichols, who was killed in Memphis, Tennessee. Five African American police officers were charged with his murder. Three Memphis fire-fighter personnel were terminated because they failed to render aid to Tyre Nichols. Two of the three are African American. I can't help but wonder have my people become like minded with white people who uses oppression for power and authority as a doorway to disobey civil rights. However, their oppressive behavior is under the disguise of making people of color obey the law.

Again, I ask the question: Will Black and Brown people become the oppressors to aid in the perpetuation of systemic racism? For some reason this is a painful reality for Black, Brown, and White people. You may not want to answer this question, but you need to. Here are some lines.

_____

_____

How do you feel?

_____

_____

You know when we acknowledge our true feelings, we begin to live a life of truth. Sometimes the truth is painful; however, pain can be liberating.

Speaking of pain, God's heart will be in pain when the world becomes more robotic. Why? God, our Creator, created the world for humanity to dwell in and to have dominion over. Unfortunately, humanity will try to become like the Creator in their own way by creating a world of robots. In other words, God created humanity, in turn, humanity creates humanoid robots. Where is the irony? Do you see it?

_____

_____

I believe the Critical Race Theory isn't a threat to society. On the other hand, the Human Replacement Theory is a threat to the extinction of humanity. Why do I believe? I am a prophet of the foretold; therefore, God told me this will happen. Do you believe it? Do you receive it?

_____

We can prolong our extinction percentage by not supporting every advancement in technology especially when it comes to humanoid robots. I value my relationships with friends and family. Robots can't give me the same affection. Unfortunately, humanity won't know what they will be missing because relationships with humanoid robots will become a way of life. Working side by side with a robot will be intriguing and rewarding. They will increase productivity, accurateness and require less wages. Businesses won't have to be consumed with vacation, sick, bereavement, and maternity leave human workers. Humanoid robots will be a win-win investment, but a lose-lose for humanity. Government assistance will run out because of its demand and not enough supply. The futuristic thought of Social Security becoming obsolete will come to pass. Laws will be enforced to protect the humanoid robots. They will be given more rights than humans because we will be the minority. Additionally, since the country is going to be led by more robots, their freedoms and rights will be protected.

I know that I've said a lot. Let's process it here:

_____

_____

_____

Again, how are you feeling??

_____

_____

_____

Really, who would have thought humanity will be on the verge of becoming extinct in the vast future?

When we try to create a futuristic world of existence, we fail. We aren't God but made in the image of God. What does "made in the image of God" really mean? Here is a synopsis for John Wesley, who is the founder of the Methodist denomination:

> *Great question! Humans are created in the image of God (Genesis 1:27), which means we were created good. We are made to be in a close relationship with God — to love God and love our neighbor, who is also created in the image of God. It also means God gave us some responsibility to be God's representatives in the world, to be the caretakers of God's creation.*
>
> *In an early sermon called "The Image of God," Wesley describes pre-fall humanity as having "an unerring understanding, an uncorrupt will, and perfect freedom" and God gave "the last stroke to the image of God in man, by crowning all these with happiness."*
>
> *Happiness is part of the image of God! Sin then enters, distorting that image in us, but it is still there. Wesley writes, "The instrument being now quite untuned" — God's image is still there, but we are not in tune with it. God restores that image in us through God's sanctifying grace"[2]*

The creation story allows us to see how God created the heavens, the earth and all that dwells in it, including humanity. God wants us to be good stewards. It's up to us to take care of the earth. We are expected to do good to all that God has given us. When God sees we can take care of a little, God will give us more – bless us abundantly. Unfortunately, because of our greed, we have become selfish human beings, who lack for nothing but want everything even if it's at the cost of mistreating and abusing others.

The free will of power has eluded us to wanting more and more. Therefore, we substitute the will of God for the will of Satan, but we can't serve two masters. We will love one and hate the other. Satan knows God is displeased with the actions of humanity, but humanity won't stop because of the will to be disobedient or sin. Thanks be to God for sending Jesus as the sacrificial lamb so that we can repent, be forgiven, and work to not sin in that way again. We'll never be perfect; however, we must keep striving for Christian perfection.

Thank you Lord for your love, grace, and mercy!!

---

[2] https://www.umc.org/en/content/ask-the-umc-what-is-meant-by-the-term-image-of-god

CHAPTER TEN

CONCLUSION

As I am concluding this journal, my heart saddens at what the world will become. I won't be living on earth when humanoid robots assist in leading our country. Thus, God did tell me that I will come to lead the remnant of humans to the land flowing with milk and honey. The land where the grass will be green, the waters are mirror clear, the sky is heavenly blue, and the soil is ripe.

The birth of a new world of people will take place. Will it be more Black and Brown people? The Lord said *Yes*. Fortunately, there will be white people too because the Holy Spirit will connect them to rebirth their race. Whites will still be the minority and will lose much of their power and authority.

The world will be recreated again with the help of our Lord and Savior. Jesus will show humanity how to fish for food, build homes with his carpenter skills, teach the love of God, and how to love others unconditionally. He will tell stories about his parents. We will know more about his earthly father (Joseph), Mary, and his siblings because he will tell the stories to those dwelling on the new land. However, Jesus won't tell them who he is; but they will figure it out since someone will have an olive grey and black tattered bible. I saw it in my vision. They held the bible captive because the stories gave them hope while they waited on hope to rescue them from war and destruction.

With this being said, for the last of humanity to have a bible in their possession, we need to pass one down from generation to generation. We also need to preserve history by putting historical books in a fireproof safe. Then make sure we continue to teach each generation to read especially as schools become obsolete. Storytelling is essential at every gathering. It is how we learn about our ancestors, remedies, and history. The heart-wrenching part of this prophecy is to know schools won't be a necessity for humans. Imagine a world in which daycares, preschools, elementary, middle, high, and secondary schools have become almost obsolete. Education will be a choice not a force. Employment will be scarce. There will be manufacture jobs in which people will learn from on-the-job experience. Priority and prominent careers will be for those who can manufacture, maintain, and operate humanoid robots. There will be researchers, first responders, teachers, faith leaders, but these professions will be at minimum capacity. These occupations will be necessary for the continuous production of humanoid robots.

Human life will look quite different. Future generations might not get a wholistic view of humanity's life because the development of artificial intelligence will encompass history books. Social media will decline. Printed photographs will go adrift; and yet some will be discovered from preservation. Scientists will excavate burial sites to learn more about human and animal existence. They will wonder how we reproduced at a rapid rate, and then become almost extinct. For they won't know sex between a male and female is the rapid answer. However, God will raise up a prophet among them, who will have visions and be led by the Holy Spirit to help God rebirth humanity. I know you are thinking: *God doesn't need any help to rebirth humanity because Adam was formed from the dust of the earth.* The reason is: it's God's will. Sometimes, we don't completely understand the will of God until after the task has been complete.

When it's time for us to reflect on our journey, the Holy Spirit will help us gain a clearer understanding. I have been on a journey with you while writing in your journal. You may be in belief, disbelief, or somewhere in between. I am broken at the thought of what will take place. Although, I am overjoyed to know Jesus will come to bring light and life to a broken world. Therefore, when the second Bible is written, and humanity's history is recorded again we will understand more about the second coming. But, we won't be alive on earth but dwelling in heaven or hell. Our future generation will read about the preexistence of their ancestors like we are discovering ours today on ancestry.com and other genealogy companies.

As followers of Jesus, I ask you to help people to value their existence, teach them patience and love. We have to stop always wanting things done rapidly for instant gratification. We also have to develop a relationship with our neighbors. The more we become secluded from each other, the more we won't miss authentic and loving relationships. Therefore, keep teaching the two greatest commandments:

You must love the Lord your God with all your heart, with all your being, and with all your mind. This is the first and greatest commandment. And the second is like it: You must love your neighbor as you love yourself... (Matthew 22:37-39).

Well, my brothers and sisters in Christ, it's time for me to leave you now. God isn't giving me much to say except, *It's up to humanity on how long it will take for my Son to return to my created kingdom.*

I know that I've mentioned some controversial topics and gave you much to reflect on. Sometimes, it's challenging for us to believe our beliefs and actions aren't Christlike. This journal wasn't my own doing – But God's! I began to writing the journal as a book; however, God told me to write it as a reflection journal. Hopefully, you were able to ponder, reflect, discern, and cherish the time spent on answering the questions.

I would like for you to treasure this journal and pass it to the next generation so that they will know what happened to their ancestors. Also, keep birth certificates, marriage licenses, and a family tree in a fireproof safe and pass it down. Whenever it is discovered, there will be evidence of you and your family's existence. Your life matters!

May the Lord be with you.

Blessings,
Reverend Tondala L. Hayward
A Prophet of the Foretold

REFLECTIONS
